The Dead Pets Poetry Anthology

Damian Ward Hey
& Rick C. Christiansen
Editors

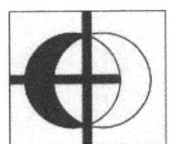

TRANSCENDENT ZERO PRESS
HOUSTON, TEXAS

Copyright © 2023, Transcendent Zero Press.

PUBLISHED BY TRANSCENDENT ZERO PRESS
www.transcendentzeropress.com

All right reserved. No portion of this book may be reproduced whether in print or electronic format without exclusive written permission from the publisher Transcendent Zero Press, or of the respective authors as represented in this anthology.

ISBN: 978-1-946460-43-1

The Dead Pets Poetry Anthology

**Damian Ward Hey
& Rick C. Christiansen**
Editors

For Annie and Bennington.

For them all.

Table of Contents

Introduction
Damian Ward Hey   13

Maria Nazos
Annie's Ghazal   15

Sandra Anfang
Yoda: A Remembrance   16

Catherine Arra
Between Us and Them   18

Madeline Artenberg
Namesake   19

Lucinda Atkins
Donatello   20

Lana Hechtman Ayers
For Rainy Day, My Greyhound   22

Christine A. Barbour
Calico Memories   23

Tina Barry
Here Lies Butch   24

Rachel Baum
The Last Fire Tower   25

Ruth Bavetta
The Dog Knows   26

Shelly Blankman
Missing Gizmo   27

Eric Chiles
Beebe   28

Rick C. Christiansen
Into the Can 30
Ode to a Hound Who Is Failing 31

Jane Connelly
The Screen Door 32

Lynda V. E. Crawford
Scamper 33

Megan Dausch
Last Moments 34

Dave Day
Karmic Canidae 35

Robert L. Dean, Jr.
One Fine Fall Day Mr. Pickles Makes a Cameo 36

Jane Desmond
Veterinary Lessons 37

Shane Dickie
The Last Days of Ralph 40

Linda Trott Dickman
Kirby 41
This Haunted House 42

Sara Kass Eifler
Burying My Cat 43

Mary Belardi Erickson
Pet Store Turtle 44

Gerry Fabian
One Field Too Many 46

Lee Eric Freedman
End 48

Linda McCauley Freeman
The Hole Where My Heart Used to Be		49
Waiting		50

Audrey Friedman
Ice is growing up the wall		52

Charlotte Friedman
Gone		53

Marianne Gambaro
Felinus Hereticus		55
Schrödinger's Kitten		56

Roberta Gould
Elegy for My Dog, Lily		58

Lola Haskins
Elegy for Woolah		59

Vali Hawkins-Mitchell
STUPID STUPID STUPID BIRD		60

Damian Ward Hey
Elegy for Bennington		61

Patricia Hope
For Sunny (1997-2005) and Cody (1996-2012)		62
Icicles of Anguish		63

Lydia Horvath
Resting Place		64

Amy Karon
For Baloo, One Month Later		65

Karen Kilcup
Requiem		66

Laurie Kolp
Playing Games		67

Rick Lupert
Filled Up   68

Bernadette Martonik
Sand   70

Glen A. Mazis
Bhakti, the Zen Chihuahua   71

Joan Mazza
Time to Say Goodbye   72

Shallene McGrath
Lost Pets   73

Robin Michel
After Seventeen Years   74
The Angel Fish We Called Paco   76

Felicia Mitchell
When a Cat Decides to Leave   77

Suzanne Morris
A Blue Shroud   78
Last Words of a Border Collie   80

Alice Campbell Romano
I Killed Our Dog   81

Ruth Sabath Rosenthal
Baby Talk   82

Phip Ross
A Lesson after De-Worming   83
Dogged   84
Fetch   85

Alice Sanford
Death and Resurrection   86

Lauren Scharhag
The Ledger — 87
Jack & Lucy — 88

Karen Scott
Heaven? — 89
Tadger at Sixteen — 90
Transition — 92

Emily Simmons
Everything but the Horse — 93

Kashiana Singh
My Brother's Dog, Laika — 94

Jess Skyleson
Looking Back — 97

Kristyn Snedden
Murphy's Requiem — 98

Betty Stanton
Leaving Stones — 100

Joseph Stanton
Cat — 101

Claire Taylor
September, Again — 103

Ingrid L. Taylor
Haunting — 104
How Far We Could Run — 105

Peter Taylor
Dog Reincarnate — 107

Alarie Tennille
Sisters — 109

Kerry Trautman
Dead Cats   110
Stray III   112

Mark Tulin
A Tonkinese Pedigree   113
Remnants of You   114

Alan Walowitz
Ghost-Cat   115

Amy Sage Webb-Baza
Feet   117

Kathleen Weed
Absence (For Flora)   118

Laura Grace Weldon
Open Like Hands   119
This German Shepherd   120

Jon Wesick
Stay   121

Fred Zirm
First Walk without My Dog   122
Undiscovered Country   123

Contributor Bios   **124**

Introduction from the Editor of *Stone*

On the day before Christmas Eve, 2021, my parents' dog, Bennington, ran into the road in front of their mountain home in upstate New York and was hit by a car. We like to think he was killed instantly. This makes it easier for us. Bennington's death was untimely. I'm not a magical thinker, but I cannot help but believe that his violent end was somehow not what was meant to be. As I write in the poem that appears in this volume, Bennington was hit by a car that "knocked him into ghost." I don't think he knew what hit him, and I imagine it took him a bit to realize he was dead.

At nearly the same time, my friend and fellow poet, Rick C. Christiansen, also lost a pet. His beloved Basset Hound, Annie, had succumbed to cancer. He wrote a poem about her, as I had about Bennington. Reading each other's poems, one of us suggested, half-joking, that we put together a whole anthology of dead pet poems. We laughed, but we also realized what a powerful and cathartic idea this was. Within a day or two, Rick put together a call for submissions, and I posted it on the homepage of *Stone Poetry Journal*.

We received hundreds of submissions. Evidently, the topic of dead pets had struck a chord with many people. It's not hard to see why. Pets are an integral part of our families and our lives. And they pass from us very quickly. They break our hearts, and yet we wouldn't trade the opportunity to love them for anything in the world.

Here's the question: Who in the world would want to buy and read an anthology of poetry devoted to dead pets? I've considered this throughout the volume's entire selection and editing process. I believe that people read poetry to help themselves work through and heal from the problems and tragedies of their lives. It may not be easy to read through the collection of poems in this volume, but the poems included within are nothing if not cathartic. We humans are social creatures. When we mourn, we reach out. We seek the company of others who have mourned as we have. The narrator of A.E. Houseman's poem, "Terence, This Is Stupid Stuff," advises us to read poetry — rather than numb our pain with intoxicants — in order to deal with life's troubles:

…take it: if the smack is sour,
The better for the embittered hour;
It should do good to heart and head
When your soul is in my soul's stead…

Taken in small, consistent doses, Houseman's poem suggests, poetry helps inure us to life's pain and suffering.

In his "Preface to *The Lyrical Ballads*," Wordsworth famously defines poetry as "the spontaneous overflow of powerful feeling: it takes its origin from emotion recollected in tranquility." The poems in this anthology are precisely that — with or without the tranquility. Some of them are humorous; some are heart-breaking.

All of the poems included here are viscerally human — because we humans have written them in celebration of the pets that we loved and cared for, and that loved and cared for us. It is fitting, therefore, that all profits made by sales of this anthology be donated to animal welfare charity.

Damian Ward Hey
Editor-in-Chief
Stone Poetry Quarterly (www.stonepoetryjournal.com)

Maria Nazos
Annie's Ghazal
—for Annie Christiansen, RIP, 3/22/2022

Not just a dog or poem. Not just dead. Today, she's your memory
waking you late at night to take her out, reminding you, not yet a memory —

At 2 am, nudging you from arthritic dreams. For a minute, you'd forget
your bad hip. Half-asleep, walking her in Missouri rain, her old body, an enemy

that continues to begrudge itself. Does anyone have a love they've not
put to rest? If not, fuck them all, this poem is for you, and for everyone

who's lost someone, anyone, they've loved. Your granddaughter petted
her long ears one last time, Said, *you'll go to sleep, please, remember me—*

The best way you can love someone is to put them down to rest,
before they fail and fall so deeply, they're stripped of any dignity.

You: born to a mother who held your head underwater during baths,
your tiny body flailing, trying to breathe, your hair an anemone.

Still, you pushed through, group homes and steel bars, set aside firearms.
Grew into a father, fell in love, divorced, fell in love, and now write poetry

Before you set her free, you held her on the table. Did her dewy eyes
realize that death is sometimes what we're left, our only remedy?

And even as your house stands silent, there's a hound, somewhere, late
at night, begging a man to let her out — and her name is Annie.

Sandra Anfang
Yoda: A Remembrance

Archimage, dreadlocks formed
where you stopped grooming;
shriveled beneath our vigilance
only fur and bones remained.

As the muscle, flesh departed
your appetite and cry grew stouter.
You would caterwaul for food
hounding us to the can opener.

In a single day
you made your contemplated leap —
as though down from some garden wall —
from world to underworld.

I shut my eyes
bleed tears into pillows
but frames of you keep floating by
like seaweed tendrils.

Spirit won't settle in your bed
the essence of your three-pound body
wafting up through musty earth
refuses to succumb.

I try again for sleep
but poems convene
like bumblebees in ceanothus
spreading twenty-three-year gossip.

These last few months
you'd hunker by me on the couch
an elfin shadow miming me
a maiden aunt awaiting tea.
You'd not be caught dead there
in your youth
canvassing the hood

cat boys at your side.

But lately, sweet remembrance
we held hands shyly
like the roots of old redwoods
twining underground.

Catherine Arra
Between Us and Them

a blizzard today, the first of winter,
late for even the ground hog.

I've braised a hearty stew, baked a pumpkin pie.
He spent daybreak writing, now naps.

Perhaps this fourth season, frantic
and silent, will help us mend a new fracture,
swallow the rawness again.

This time not a father, a grandmother. A dog,
Kugie, broken in a squirrel chase. The car
unable to stop its red or the death howl.

He's only a dog, we know.
Panama and Jemmie only cats. It's only snow,
this blizzard.

The white will melt and give way, gather us in drifts,
freeze until spring when we will know better

how to live in two houses
and run between them a snowy bridge.

Madeline Artenberg
Namesake

Father always listens to Mother.
In dreams, he plays poker, goes
bowling, feels the "Attaboy, Harry"
slaps on his back.

Finally, a bowling-league nephew
kidnaps him. Shoes on, giddy,
he steps up to the line—an old,
first-timer. He throws the ball
low. It does a slow-mo
down the gutter.

Face reddening, he throws
the second ball high: strike!
He crumples onto the alley: stroke!
Lies there, pulse fading
inside his living dream.

Mourning over, I finally get
my first pet: a hermit crab.
For a year, I watch him run
across the rug, tell him stories
of his namesake, Harry.

Going on vacation, I leave a large shell
next to his small one plus plenty of water
and carrots for days. I return to an empty
exoskeleton, next to his desiccated, little,
pink body lying in front of the entrance
to his big, new home.

Lucinda Atkins
Donatello

About as big as a teacup,
saucer eyes,
no tail to speak of.
Bear? No ma,
Donatello.
Velvet brown,
almost black,
sucks on the corner of
my apron,
cringes at the Hoover,
breathes in concert with the boy.
Scoots his ass across the
den rug until it wears out
in that particular spot....
must smell like
a piece of heaven
he says, jesting
as he lets him out
and I reach for the sponge .

Paws on the window sill
watching 60 by 100.
Squirrel.
SQUIRREL.
Snow.
Squirrel.
Green.
SQUIRREL.
Back door,
a world of hostas.
Dog's years.
Come home.
Come home and see him.
Oldest dog
in the practice
he says as
he slides in the needle.

Good boy
good boy
baby boy
he whispers
Donny boy.

Lana Hechtman Ayers
For Rainy Day, My Greyhound
(May 4, 2008—October 14, 2021)

Is it a trick of shadow
or memory's insistence
that I spy you
out of the corner of my eye?

Sleek as a deer, majestic as a lion.
The color of shadow yourself,
except for your smile,
bright as looking into the sun too long,
an afterimage burned onto my heart.
Tip of your tongue hanging out
like a little pink heart itself.

You're shaking off sleep,
perhaps a dream of running,
to prance toward your water fountain
and quench what must be
death's eternal thirst.

You can't be here, of course,
but even after my eyes adjust
to your absence,
the jingle of unseeable collar tags,
rings and rings and rings
like a bell calling me to morning prayer.

Christine A. Barbour
Calico Memories

As I held your wasting body on my lap
and felt your urine ebb out onto my jeans,
I knew that soon you would be merely a mix
of calico memories.

In the vet's office, you let me know you were
scared and hurting when you delivered
your final bite and blood dripped out
from my forefinger in a perfectly round
red spot as another fluid,
that would take your ninth life,
eased into your almost non-existing
vein.

On the long walk back to the car,
I felt that you were in the carrier.
I could not tell because your body
was so light, as if your marrow
had dried up and left only
hollow bones.

So, except for the lack
of your sound – long spread-out tracks
of meow, like with Schrödinger's cat
after the vial is broken,
there is a fifty percent chance of you
being here or not here when I open
the carrier at home.

Tina Barry
Here Lies Butch

We hated to lose Butch, but he was ancient
and ready to die, his eyes milky marbles, multi-tasking
tail that fanned our feet, dragged like a dead branch.

Like every morning, Butch stalled in front
of our neighbor's house to pee on the forsythias,
then passed, lips smirked over black-streaked teeth.

My wife and me in blurry misery, drank
whisky while I shoveled a hole
in our yard's spring-damp soil.

Nothing is sadder than a mound
of dirt with something dead beneath it,
so we drove to Lowe's, returned

with a dozen Day-lilies. The flowers,
ruffled ticker-tape parades
of lime and purple.

Butch would have whined with pleasure
over the colors. They matched his favorite knit
blanket, and we had buried him in that.

Rachel Baum
The Last Fire Tower

I remember the steep woods the rocky world
My dog and I danced where ground fog curled
A backcountry hike in the shadowed afternoon
Awnings of snow above us like infinite moon

Past blackened branches an abandoned lean-to
Narrow places he poured his liquid body through
The skim of breeze as he raced brave ahead
First to reach the tower a laddered woodshed

We climbed fearlessly high enough to fly
Stood on its platform and implored the sky
To not forget this moment this fortunate hour
This small spirit a glint of bright sun in a snow shower

And so view the horizon from lookout to evergreen
A reminder of time and trails unseen
Then claim the final mountain the last fire tower
This was recklessness. This was valor.

Ruth Bavetta
The dog knows

when you're in a sulk
sitting on the bottom step.
She comes from the back,
smelling of tomato leaves
and fresh cut grass, a stray twig
caught in her shaggy skirts.

She's been eating tomatoes again,
and chasing mockingbirds
through the orange trees. The black mud
of the ditches covers her white paws.

She pushes her long, crooked nose
into your armpit and suddenly
the desire to bury your face
deep in her white ruff overwhelms you.

Even the prick of the leaves,
from where she's been rolling
under the sweetgum, revives
your secret belief
that every ache can be cured.

Shelly Blankman
Missing Gizmo

You disappeared into the darkness five years ago.
I don't know why. People say you were only a cat
and that's what cats do. But you weren't just a cat.

Cats don't shred calendars or stash eyeglasses under
a bed. They don't steal pizza or chow mein from the plates
of their humans or drink from their straws, and they don't hitch

rides on the hips of dogs six times their size. You'd greet me
each morning by leaping on my shoulder, sleep by my side
whenever I was down, draw blood with your nips whenever

we would play and then look at me innocently like a child
as if to say, "What did I do?" when you knew. I'd just laugh, and
you knew I'd do that, too. You'd lick my tears dry and when

I was sick, you'd curl your body around my neck like a scarf,
and stay with me until I'd fall asleep to the lullaby of your purrs.
But you were sick. Almost from the time you rescued me.

Maybe at some point, you'd had enough of vets' visits; I'll
never know. We hired two search dogs to find you, posted
ads, knocked on doors, cruised neighborhoods. Nothing.

Still, I wait. Every time I leave the house. Each corner I turn,
each yard I pass, I look for you. Each bush that rustles I hope
it's you — exhausted, starved, desperate to find your way home.

After two years, I am still waiting ….

Eric Chiles
Beebe

Years ago my wife and children
wanted to breed our Springer spaniel.
We eventually sold all the litter of eight
except the runt. We named her Beebe.

Her left eye wandered in its socket.
Roscoe, the last brother to leave,
sensing she wasn't right,
would snarl and attack,
biting her neck.
Separating them risked
getting nipped by the savage
pup's needle-like teeth.

Pets mean yellow
puddles on the floor.
But poor Beebe had a
liver and white charm,
a smiling mouth, wagging tail,
that made me pat her head.

Before her first birthday,
she started to limp.
Then she couldn't move
a rear leg. Within a week
she couldn't get up
from her green plaid blanket bed.
The vet found an inoperable
tumor in her spinal cord.

I visited her before she got
the fatal needle.
She lay on a urine-stained
white towel on a cold steel tray.
She could only move
her sad, good eye.
Tearing up, I patted her,

said goodbye and removed
her small red collar.

Now when I go to the garage
to get the lawnmower,
her name tag jingles
from the fading collar hung
on a nail by the door.

Rick C. Christiansen
Into the Can

The small black kitten has been crushed, not yet quite dead. Her dark eyes are slits in her flattened face. Her white teeth are showing through her opened mouth, the tip of her pink tongue rests on the teeth, slightly protruding. She is trembling with small convulsions. I hold her in my 10 year old hands, ask my stepfather, almost pleading, if we can take her to the doctor. *"No point"*, he says. *"She's trash now, put her in the can outside."* I walk up the steps from our basement apartment cradling the kitten in my upturned palms. I can still feel her trembling. I reach the heavy gray metal trash can. With the kitten in the crook of one arm, I pry off the frozen lid. I place the kitten onto the mound of cardboard and garbage in the can. It is twilight. Her black form lays on its side on the cardboard, like a charcoal cameo. I slowly replace the lid.

some need to grow thorns
to touch the pearl drop waters
part of me falls through

"Into the Can" was previously published in *MacQueen's Quinterly*, Issue 11, January 1, 2022.

Rick C. Christiansen
Ode to a Hound Who Is Failing

First—
She is a *who,* not a *what*—personality manifest
stubbornness and affection. A spirit soft and malleable
as her long velvet ears.

Grunts as a pup evolved into the groans of age.
Neither a complaint, both an assertion of effort
born from instinct, honed by character.
Life is a target.

Like chasing a rabbit on the run, everything
is focused on the try. I watch her hips
waver climbing the stairs. An errant foot
cascading to the side and then:

recovery of balance that reclaims dignity.
She is not mournful, only determined
to remain herself through the entropy.
Cataract squint across the room to see

what has already been discerned by
a nose that will NEVER fail. More groans
to rise and greet, as the lady of the manor,
all those who come to her home.

She is always welcoming—accepting
of all that join her space. Her hunting
mellowed to a search for friends.
Magnanimous instinct no more discerning prey.

I think she knows that *she* is now hunted.
Age overtakes her once swift stride and
ambles beside her. Ready to strike—
I hope death is patient as I am not ready.

She is ready for anything that comes.
A lifetime of calm acceptance—she will
accept her last visitor as she has greeted
everyone before: with gentle attention.

Jane Connelly
The Screen Door

I sit at the back door with Luigi
My cat, who has aged along with me, and
Who may be the last of my pets
He stares out, as he often does, to the
Corner of the yard where his brother,
Aloysius, sleeps under the earth.

The statue I placed there looks
Exactly like him, and that was where
Luigi saw me carry him away
Out of the house we all shared for years.

As quickly as events change our lives
The weather changed overnight, and the
Wind is bending the tops of the sycamore trees
Back and forth, as if in prayer
Clapping the branches, and the
Colorful leaves are falling, falling
Covering the yard and the grave.

The wind rattles the screen door
And for a moment I hear Aloysius
Scratching at the screen door once again.

"The Screen Door" was previously published in *Bard's Review,* 2020.

Lynda V. E. Crawford
Scamper

Were you running to freedom
when you dashed through the door

tiny black body nursed
from birth—not by your mother
soft white teeth falling out as
I pushed a bottle of cow's milk in?

You must have needed one scamper
into space unstressed
from the weight of curried oxtails
chopped onions, browning

un-trapped by walls that separate
living from sleeping, cooking from eating.

I cried for you, my bleeding pup
in my clutch, shitting unknowing
across my gut, your back crushed.

In the moments before brakes crunched
we were both happiest.

Megan Dausch
Last Moments

Your strength guided me for nine years, but your job was not done.
You took on tending mom through her
illness. Bones creaking,
nails tapping; her audible shadow.
When it was time, you waited
until everyone you loved stood
with hearts and hands wrapped around you.

You waited until my young guide dog curled into your side. Bodies
so close your pelts blended.
Quiet protected you like a shell;
we watched in reverence.
They say a dog is just a dog, but I know
your body pressed instructions
into his galloping youthful heart.
Maybe you even laughed.
"Worry is her middle name," you said.
"Remember to sniff some turkey every once in a while," you advised.

And when you were finished doling out advice, you rose.
Walked on shaking legs to your new master, my dad.
He knew without words, you had done your job.
Done what all life needs to do. You made this world
a better place.
On your favorite bed in my parents' living room you
sipped one last breath of this sweet world.
My hand rested on your back,
light as air.
Years have unspooled faster than spring thunderstorms, but
your paws always tick softly,
on the ever-growing surface of my heart.

Dave Day
Karmic Canidae

Linoleum icy cold
blinding fluorescent light, my stomach

fucking hurts. So good to see you, let's
go home for the love of god. Yes, yes

always the cameraphones, the smell of
pockets, thoroughly uninterested, I shudder

the vet. Warmer and warmer, faces fade away
halcyon halftones—kudzu, squirrel, sofa

peanut, piano, tennis ball, am I still
awake? The flavor of water all consuming

memories fizzle into fathomless pure white
I sniff the void and time crystallizes.

I blink my eyes open and inhale my
mother whole, soul unblemished, taste the

milk once, then twice. Squeaky rubber and grass
how wonderful to be young on planet earth!

Robert L. Dean, Jr.
One Fine Fall Day Mr. Pickles Makes a Cameo

John's Animal World
has closed its doors. Ridden,
gut shot, into the sunset. Ahead

looms winter like the Teton massif.
Road kill litters the highway.
Geese explode lake calm,

skim the mirror's surface.
Seared against the beetling sky
reflections swarm like gnats.

Caught in the spokes
of memory, a hamster
lies, twitching.

Come back, John.
Come back.

"One Fine Fall Day Mr. Pickles Makes a Cameo" first appeared in *Shot Glass Journal*, issue #26, Sept. 2018.

Jane Desmond
Veterinary Lessons

Yesterday,
at the vet's,
I learned how to
puncture
your skin,

to pull your wild, soft fur
up
like a tent
between your shoulder blades,
behind your tall, tufted, bunny ears
that make you look
perpetually surprised,

to prick the tiny needle in
and wait
while the thin plastic tube,
looping like a twirl of linguine,
fills
with clear liquid from the bulging pouch:

Just the right balance of electrolytes
to help your kidneys
keep flushing toxins.

This will now be
our daily routine--
a solution
to keep you
alive…

Slowly,
a balloon of that water
bulges
under your thin skin
with its plush angora coat
pushing

slate colored fur
out
like a fuzzy softball.

Then,
like a magician's trick,
it subsides,
life-giving fluids
sucked up
by your tissues.

I pluck the needle out —
short, thin, — a minor thing,
and, treatment done,
know that

"When the time comes,"
(as the veterinarian puts it,)
when your kidneys fail,
no matter how much water
is pushed through them,

another needle,
longer-wider-but just as sharp
will deliver a different solution.

Bright blue juice from the doctor's hand
will be your final treatment:
your death a quiet endless sleep.

When my time comes,
when pain grinds all away but a tiny glimmer
of who I used to be
I wish such a simple solution
could be brought to bear:

a glide of surgical tip,
beveled steel slid into my vein
the warming plunge of bright blue toxins
to still my heart:

suffering's
generous
end.

"Veterinary Lessons" first appeared in *The Intima: A Journal of Narrative Medicine*, in their Fall, 2019 issue."

Shane Dickie
The Last Days of Ralph

Ralph the mole lived in our house in a tiny hole.
At night I could hear him gnawing with his sharp teeth,
While I sat comfortably in my lounge chair,
Resting my feet.
Ralph had it good, Ralph had it grand,
Ralph was the king of the moles in his Popsicle stand.
Not a care in the world had Ralph,
With the comfort of the roaring fire and the thunder
Of the piano upstairs; Ralph had it made and he knew it.
But time was short and Ralph was not long for this world.
So Ralph reveled in his digs as much as a mole could,
And one day Ralph's time was up. The good Lord took him.
So long Ralph… May your teeth be always sharp to gnaw with and
May your chatter always be chipper.

Linda Trott Dickman
Kirby
— *for our opinionated Coton' du Tulear*

You are:
A mixture of cultured
and wild rogue canine
a curmudgeon with a heart
a reluctant snuggler
an acrobat
a tunneler
a friend
Tenacious defender of everything — especially our daughter.
We nod to your royal roots
celebrate your marriage into the wild
love you who loves to pretend.
We lay you to rest
with wood from Narcissus
with wood from Second
with a fleur de lis,
We commend your Spirit oh
opinionated pup who sailed into our hearts from Huntington Bay
and sails out with the tide.
Fair winds and a following sea...

Linda Trott Dickman
This Haunted House

In the upstairs hallway
Just inside the closet
A working man's sweat leaks
into the night air. I cringe, always.
Just beyond, the sound of mom bumping into the altered wall
every morning, on her way
to that first quiet cup.
On the landing, I hear Jacque's puppy nails dancing toward a door that
no longer keeps him in.
The mahogany table has expanded beyond its wooden insert.
Four generations of radio days, family plays, welcomings, partings
reunions, estrangements
secrets, pasta and meatballs
bathed in wine by the cook's hands. Full to spilling over, the thin
mahogany veneer always protected.
There's no place like home.

Sara Kass Eifler
Burying My Cat

A strange light descends.
The wind is punishing
and clean. I choose a place
by a tree
in our backyard.
Next to the downed branch
from this summer's
big storm.

The grass is stringy,
tough. The shovel cuts it
awkwardly. I scrape
a root raw, dig
further. The earth is rich
and black
and then sandy,
dry. Then
soft clay.

Earlier, you were with me.
Earlier, much earlier,
we two curled together
and did not separate.

But now there is the soil.
The ground I dig hollow.
Now there is the wind, the light.
Now, the tree,
watching.

Mary Belardi Erickson
Pet Store Turtle

You can't pet a turtle
like you can a cat or dog,
but I can tell you
I found my heart soft
for a small Asian turtle
purchased because my son
was allergic to fur pelt.
At first, he listened
from his bed
to his turtle's nocturnal rambles.
After the boy declared
his Turtle's lunching
on goldfish too noisy,
I moved it to a smaller tank
in our living room.
I fed it reptile pellet food,
kept the light positioned
over its sunning rock.
It had a white ceramic bowl
for soaking while I cleaned its tank.
Always, I washed any muck
from its back and underside.
It learned the routine
did not panic quite as much
upon my approach.
Early on, it had escaped once.
My son had found it drying-out
and covered with dust-bunnies.
A pet turtle lives a quiet life
in a glass tank, until after years
it is suddenly gone.
I wrapped ours in plastic
for the shed refrigerator--
until my son was home
and buried Turtle

in our pet cemetery
where then we said a few words
in praise of turtles.

"Pet Store Turtle" was first published in *Waterways: Poetry in the Mainstream*, July 2012, Vol. 33, no.2.

Gerry Fabian
One Field Too Many

In late autumn, the spaniel
eyes the distant meadow.
I reluctantly give in.
We walk the thistled meadow
where we have hunted
since he was a pup.

I bring the Remington shotgun
more for appearance
than practical purpose.

I unleash the dog
who lopes into the field.
Spaniels leap and bound
when they run
until hip dysplasia sets in.

He covers the field
in a crisscross pattern -
nose down, nose snorting, nose down.

To both of our surprise,
he sends up a bevy of quail.
I fire in their direction
hoping not to hit any
but I bring down two.

The dog retrieves the first one
dropping it at my feet
and bolts for the second one.
I see him go down.
Breaking into an almost run,
I reach him as he struggles
to get up but falls
and splays in yelping pain.

I hold him in my arms

and his quail blood tongue
licks my face.
As I try to carry him,
he whines an eerie
piercing howl.

Placing him back down,
I mark the spot
with some large branches
and return to the truck
for my pistol.

Lee Eric Freedman
End
— *Happie the Dog: 1972-1988*

my heart bleeds
for my friend left today
his voice lost in darkness
his silent thoughts astray

my cries of goodbye
ring out like gun shots
twisted, bloody
guts tied in knots

i tried and i tried
but i cannot see
why the hell did
he have to leave me

flowers bloom

cars go

bells ring

glass breaks

dreams are dreamt
promises broken

wounds don't heal

my life moves on
my memories return

daily

Linda McCauley Freeman
The Hole Where My Heart Used to Be
— for Gulliver, 2008-2020

I sit in your familiar places,
discover how the sun shifts over them,
something so obvious I don't know why it has taken me
eleven years and your absence to see it.

I sit in your spot,
third step up the back staircase that leads
from the kitchen and faces a low window where you
would peruse the world.

I sit at the curve
of the cold wooden stair and feel the sun warm me
as you would have, the way your little nose would
sniff the rising scent of breakfast while I ignored you,
your morning walk and your own breakfast over
and done.

My husband notices
this new habit but says nothing. He knows
I am trying to fill the hole you left, climb
my own stair.

Linda McCauley Freeman
Waiting
— for Gulliver, 2008-2020

I.
All day and all night
you cuddled
into my body under the blanket, refused
to leave my side, became backrest, footrest,
comforter.

When I coughed uncontrollably,
you looked at me
alarmed, and rested your paw
upon my chest.

On the third day you still
would not move, except
when your daddy called
to go outside.

You rushed back, ears flying, leapt
onto the bed, snuggled again,
willed me to wellness.

II.
I keep waking early
to walk the dog,
but there is no dog.

I keep waiting
to see his little face
as he scampers around
the corner, his nails tapping
the floorboards,

keep waiting in bed at night
for my husband
to carry him in
so I can hug him to sleep,

knowing he will leap out
after my husband
closes the door
because it is their snack time,

and he'll choose cheese
rather than my smothering arms.

I keep waiting to see him
sitting in the morning sun
on the stairs
or the green armchair
by the window,

hear him barking his head off
at the neighbor's big dog.

Next week I have surgery again.
After every other,
he snuggled
with me, helped me heal.

I am waiting.

Audrey Friedman
Ice is growing up the wall

dripping stalactites from the ceiling.
Someone I don't know pushes
my buttons. Crust of frost
melts. My relief's
brief-lived — remember
I kind of forgot
to feed the dog.
Remember I'm guilty
of her second death. I loved
her muzzle. What's happening?

Happening isn't the puzzle
I love. Me first. Death Second.
In the gilded mirror I feel that
I'm the dog, almost dead, my feed
semi-forgotten. If I hadn't remembered
that relief is but melted
frost, would crust or buttons
pushed push me to know my inside
out self that thrives
briefly beneath
a ceiling of stalactites?

The wall growls down the ice.

This poem was previously published in *Diner,* February, 2004, Vol. 4, No. 2

Charlotte Friedman
Gone

His eyes milky with age
like staring through clouds
I marveled

at the white of his fur
stripe of creme down his back
I touched my nose to his

warm and dry
drank in his breath
stroked that fine skull

for a last hour
under white fluorescents
my palm cupped his bony head

my heart slowed
to the speed of his
and the vet said *this*

is fucking hard
as she pushed
the drugs into him

and listened
for faint beating
heard nothing

nothing
my arms flew
over his body

I shrieked
called out
Maaaa

she never a comfort

and dead two years
to the day

I reached for his blue
collar silver bone-
shaped tag blue leash

I wound round
my right hand
round and round

phylacteries of blue
circling blue
as if wrapping him
around me
numbed I was
as I fumbled

for the door
for air
for breath

to stand
in rain
still

to stare
into branches
bare

Marianne Gambaro
Felinus Hereticus

Swaddled in self-righteousness,
swaying above nine-year-old heads,
the nun proclaimed that animals
do NOT have souls
and therefore canNOT go to heaven.
She saw all in black and white,
as was her habit.

With hand raised timidly,
a small voice asserted *But Sister,
it won't be heaven without my cat.*

Blasphemy!

Confounded when confronted by the logic of a child
and the loyalty and love she wore like armor for her pet,
wimple aquiver, jumbo rosary trembling from her waist
dark eyes flashing the fire of eternal, infernal damnation
she roared impotently
at the impudent girl
Be quiet and sit down.

Years later
the child-now-woman sits on the floor
holding a small gray body in her arms.
As weakening breaths come further apart,
punctuating a still steady purr,
as emerald eyes flicker
with the passing shadows of feline ancestors
all the while losing light,
one paw still in this world
and three already in the next,
she knows with certainty
that cats DO go to heaven.
She isn't so sure about nuns.

Marianne Gambaro
Schrödinger's Kitten

In the quantum-mechanical "Schrödinger's cat" paradox, according to the many-worlds interpretation, every event is a branch point; the cat in the box is both alive and dead, irrespective of whether the box is opened, but the "alive" and "dead" cats are in different branches of the universe, both of which are equally real, but which cannot interact with each other.

worry steals sleep
kitten food left untouched
blood streaked litter

this is the black cat I had always wanted
the one I thought I had gotten a decade ago
who turned out to be dark roast coffee instead
when she sat in the window
bright sun limning her fur
a sweet girl familiar
to me alone
the lovely Lilith named
for that first enchantress
who defied both God and Adam

in sleep I'd stroke her ragged ruff
and she in turn caressed
each of my fingers with raspy tongue
to dream beside me
who died too young

perhaps in some other reality
her topaz eyes still shine
her fur still glistens in the sun

but not here
now this damned kitten
keeping me awake

don't open the box

do I really want to know
if he's alive
or dead
equal realities
as long as I don't open the box
but not my choice

the tension of the mattress shifts slightly
as a small weight crawls onto my chest
relieving the weight within my chest
a gentle purr assures me
that in this branch of the universe
at least for this moment
all is well

Roberta Gould
Elegy for My Dog, Lily

Eternal window
her eyes receiving me
at last breath
through bare slits
not yet sealed
seeing me
as flesh prepares
to end
and I prepare to
imagine her presence
somewhere beyond
free to forget me finally
despite her constant faith

The empty house
we shared
I don't want it!
Walls not enough
memory to be carried
wherever I place my foot
or with each nut I crack
or the water she taught me to drink

May her infinite patience reach
and infuse me forever
and I become a viewer
of all and everything
enduring the loud and the empty
the sound of music or coyotes howling
the hand extended when needed
or offered, freely, no other than for joy

Lola Haskins
Elegy for Woolah

The dog feels a difference in their caresses.
They circle her, those three who brought her
pigs' ears and rawhide, and threw her sticks.
Her eyes are a lake in the woods, where even
the red leaves have sunk. Her left hind leg has
opened, almost joyously, as if it were saying
Look, here's bone! A stranger enters,
slides a needle in, goes. Then they are
four in the room, then three, and
a mound of fur, rising from the steel table
like an island over winter water.

"Elegy for Woolah" was published, previously, in *Asylum: Improvisations on John Clare*, University of Pittsburgh Press, 2019.

Vali Hawkins-Mitchell
STUPID STUPID STUPID BIRD

Stupid stupid stupid bird
With stupid crippled foot absurd

Hopping like a stupid toad
Trying to cross that stupid road

A stupid car just hit you smack
Your feathers blew with burst impact

Floating 'cross the stupid lane
And stupid me I gasped in pain

No more taking walks with me
How stupid that I had to see

The stupid driver didn't slow
He'd hit my bird and didn't know

My heart was crushed and eyes were blurred
O'er the stupid death of my stupid bird

Damian Ward Hey
Elegy for Bennington

So very fast, how that dog went.
Too fast for me to say his name.
So fast, it chases after him.
The car, long gone, that knocked him into ghost
discordant with the wind
before he quite knew what was what —
surely, by now, a sniff around, he's figured out.
And, if he has, he surely bears no one ill will.
I'm not a man for such belief,
and yet…
I know he'll be up at their house
for some time yet to come.
My mother may well hear his nails —
a clatter on the hardwood, now and then.
My father will be sure to note his squeals
and speech-filled growls
in the upstate New York wind that squeezes
through the cracks between the wood of their
log cabin on the mountain, in the midst of forest,
overlooking lake.
My father, the professional trombone player, says to her:
Hear that? He's made the house his mouthpiece.
And my mother, long the brass player's wife, may counter:
He's got quite a healthy embouchure.
And then, when time is right, when life has gotten
back in tune, and winds die down,
he'll scamper out into the woods, again,
to do whatever dogs will do.

Patricia Hope
For Sunny (1997-2005) and Cody (1996-2012)

Bone and sinew scattered on this tiny
sliver of earth you both loved so much. Sometimes,
I can see your smile as you and Cody waited
patiently for me to come home from work
and join you on the front porch.

At night when the wind sweeps
under the eaves and around the chimney
I can hear your yelp, picture your playful run
through the yard at Cody's side, see his leap
as he chases the birds from the forsythia bush.

The day you died he tried to escape with you
as you ran from the thunder that scared
you so. He made it across the fence but
didn't know you had reached the end
of your journey just short of that goal.

Skinned up, Cody stayed with you until
I arrived, too late to get you help. Cody
lived seven more years doing his best
to go on without you. I picture the two of you
running across endless hills, haunch-high

with sweet smelling grass, a soft breeze
blowing your fur, your ears laid back, running
toward the boat, your ride across some
heavenly lake, where love is the only thing
you know as you play together through eternity.

Patricia Hope
Icicles of Anguish

I pictured you lying somewhere, injured, dying
slowly from that frigid Friday in January, even though
we'd searched every ditch and street in the neighborhood.

All night, I sat waiting, sure if you could get home,
you'd come, scratching at the door, moaning softly as you
pressed your nose to my hand, begging for forgiveness.

I watched through cold glass for any movement,
remembered our bond, knowing you were out there
somewhere, waiting for me, like I'd waited for you.

Before I could find you, your spirit winged
to a higher place, leaving me with icicles
of anguish even now on this hot July Day.

Lydia Horvath
Resting Place

Native Ohio asters' blooms
long since faded, dropped;
even their remnants
blown away

Leaving only the bare
and frozen Black Swamp soil
above my little dog's
thin bones

Amy Karon
For Baloo, One Month Later

Dust-tipped fur; feathered toes.
Pads ten thousand miles thick.

You lead me down side trails to delights
enriched by shared witness—

mallards dabbling in reeds,
kites wheeling overhead.

Long-legged sprinter,
lover of apples and all things round,

you catapult fences, gnaw banana peels.
Once you ate an entire citronella candle.

A decade later, you teach me to age.
Hips atrophy, pain evades pills—no matter.

Spurn rugs and fireplaces.
Head-butt the door, yank the leash.

Even your collapse, at thirteen, on an autumn beach
is absolute. Indisputable. Agonizing in its finality.

It's been a month but mornings
still crush me.

I still struggle from bed—still caress
your soft black hair in my earring box.

Your ghost curls in the corner
beseeching me to walk.

Karen Kilcup
Requiem

My gloomy mother
named you Nerd, forecast
as if to warn herself,
"He's doomed: wandering
down the road to chase
a furry caterpillar,
a cat so clueless
a bird could perch on
his back and he might not
notice—more proof
that beauty and brains
rarely come together.
How long can he last?"
Tuxedoed tom who shrunk
at thunder, who chased erratic
butterflies and swatted fluttering
blooms, when you vanished
she said, "we should assume
he's dead. No wonder!"

Laurie Kolp
Playing Games

At the end of his life,
my sweet dog Paws
got Alzheimer's.
He would go to the backdoor
and whine until I let him out,
then he'd sit and yip
at the nose-smudged window.
There he'd be staring at me,
his kind button eyes begging
to come inside right then.
Not five minutes would pass
and he'd be at the backdoor again,
out and then *let me in*
over and over again.
He was like a youthful dog
going after a ball that
was not there. Did I mention
he had dementia? Still,
Paws did not forget me.
He did not forget the sound of my car
coming into the garage.
After a trip to the store, I'd open
the door and find him waiting
to go outside and come back in again.
He did not forget to curl up at my side
each night as I read in my favorite chair,
did not forget this game of out and in
we played and how he made
me react to his every move.

Rick Lupert
Filled Up
— for Tigger

Have you ever been so filled with sadness
you literally

*No-one ever uses the word literally correctly
Including me.*

ran out of room for your guts?
My cat just died and I'm feeling it.

Look, there's my spleen and both intestines
on the shelf next to the Brautigan.

There's my pancreas and a couple of organs
I can't identify thanks to my lackadaisical

efforts in high school biology, sitting on top of
an anthology of poems written, oddly enough,

in the voice of dogs.
They say time heals all wounds.

*To hell with anyone who would use a cliche
like that in a poem, including me.*

I'm staring at the clock watching it do
what it does; waiting for this sadness to empty out.

It's a slow drain.
Earlier today I found some of his

dried throw-up in the corner of our bedroom.
I didn't have the heart to clean it up,
one of the last physical remnants of
his presence here.

I miss you Tigger.
It'll be like this for a while.

Rick Lupert, "Filled Up" *Making Love to the 50 Ft. Woman,* Rothco Press 2015

Bernadette Martonik
Sand

I have been missing my dog more
than usual lately,

I left him just over two years ago
when I left my ex.

I wanted to bring him with me to this vacation
house on the beach

but the owners don't allow pets.
I imagine all the sand he might have tracked in

after running and running like a lunatic
on the shore

like he did that time my ex was not my ex
and away in France visiting his mother

and I didn't tell him when I found out I
would probably lose our baby.

Instead, I drove to the peninsula and watched
my dog run,

shot like an arrow over the
sand that went on and on

a black blur in front of an indifferent sea,
craggily rocks cutting into oblivion
That night, we slept in the car on the side of the road
like babies.

Today, he wouldn't have been able to run that far
but he would have tried.

When my ex is away and I stay with him, I
lift him onto the bed carefully, so he doesn't cry.

I would have lifted him onto the bed if he were here now,
I wouldn't have cared if sand got everywhere.

Glen A. Mazis
Bhakti, the Zen Chihuahua

She came from Paradise, not the celestial,
but the place with black buggies
with red flags waving,
warning the twenty-first century
to slow down,
boys in rounded hats hammering quietly
using old barn wood to interlock smoothly,
tongues tied and looking stoically handsome.

Maybe, it was the Amish shining eyes
without words taught her to be still,
not barking for the first year,
but even at sixteen able to calm a room.
Big brown eyes with moons lodged in them
seemed to hold fast to a heavenly tide
guiding her serenely
through others' bustle.

Named for the love of the dog
who was the first,
the only animal to enter Nirvana,
since Yudhishthira,
gambler of kingdoms and brides,
but oh so holy,
wouldn't leave behind
his most loyal friend.
Brahman at the gates couldn't believe
he wouldn't come in without her,
until he fathomed
the depth of a dog's heart.

Joan Mazza
Time to Say Goodbye

Shrunken to half her weight, not
eating, not drinking, deaf and nearly
blind, too weak to bark to let me know
she needs to go out, she sleeps and sleeps,
doesn't lift her head when I rest my hand
on her warm body. The Vet takes
one look, says *kidney failure*, agrees
it's time. She's had food and shelter,
slept in my bed since her arrival.
Loved by many, with health-
and dental care. And no unwanted
offspring. She's had my company,
playtime with two cats. I think

I'm ready but I'm crying for my final
dog. With one last kiss to her head
while her heart's still beating, I say
Goodbye, Michi. Eyes blurred, I drive
home with radio news that doesn't
soothe. Republicans rejoice though
the end is never pretty. No meds
to ease the pain, no research for cures.
No nursing home, no grandchildren
visiting, the poor will die at home
alone or on the roadway's verge
while people look away. No one
rich to see or be much disturbed.

Shallene McGrath
Lost Pets

There comes a call
like a wind
from the thicket:

a beckon
to friends
with one ear up

when howling hap
through wintering wood
reaches the fenced-in Westie

when calico cat
catching the door ajar
crawls away into wilderness

when mixed-breed hound
unhitching without a sound
leaps over the dented tailgate

when chanting,
pleading, unreachable names
strike dumb in the distant night.

Far from family
— full of love and care,
filled with mourning loss —

a call to an ancient,
wordless world, sublime,
veiled in mist, arrayed in moss —

and sometimes,
wanderlust will triumph
over home fires and soft blankets.

and not even a treat
compares to a freedom
possessed in the fearless, feral air.

Robin Michel
After Seventeen Years

This is a poem for my cat, Pudder.
After seventeen years, I have finally learned
how to sleep with you purring in the same room.

I have fed you and changed your water,
cleaned out your litter box, and once attempted
to rescue you from a house being flea-bombed
only to find you sitting beneath a tree, silently watching me
as I came out empty-handed and coughing.

But I seldom played with you, or held you in my lap,
and only carried you when I needed to take you to the vet
or wanted to put you in the laundry room so that I could sleep
without you scratching at my door during the night.
For seventeen years, my bedroom has been off-limits.

This morning, as I write you this poem,
the hum-purr of your tiny throbbing body
is the only music I need or desire.

This morning, I woke to hear you in the litter box
placed close to my bed near your makeshift bed
upon towels prepared in case you could not climb in.

I crushed the Prednisone and mixed it with tuna.
After you ate and drank, I stroked your head and tilted it back,
and forced into your mouth the syringe of painkiller.
I listened to you purr.

As I stroked you, I avoided your back.
I did not want to again feel the bones
now visible beneath your fur, did not want to think
of the many diets prescribed for you through the years
or what this new weight loss means.

I avoided your right hip, where the bone is mostly
non-existent and the tumor is not.

How could I have not seen the lump
until the vet pointed it out?

Will you—have you—forgiven me?
What is it you say with the vibrating hum
of your body?

Today, I will go to work not knowing if tonight
I will have the gift of being able to hold you,
stroke your fur, and give you the love
I only discovered after seventeen years,
in this, the last days of your long life.

"After Seventeen Years" was first published in *Our Last Walk, Using Poetry for Grieving and Remembering Our Pets*, by Louis Hoffman, Michael Moats, and Tom Greening (University Professors Press, 2016.)

Robin Michel
The Angel Fish We Called Paco

floats upward to the light
from which we all radiate.

As his fins spread into wings
he is transformed and reborn
into his rightful name.

A glimpse of heaven lingers
on his artificial sea —

Robin Michel "After Seventeen Years" *Our Last Walk, Using Poetry for Grieving and Remembering Pets,* University Professor's Press 2016

Felicia Mitchell
When a Cat Decides to Leave
— In Memory of Charles the Cat

When a cat decides to leave,
all birds fly away home
to get there before he passes.
They pull their shutters tight
but leave a crack to watch,
curious, as curious about cats
as cats are about birds, in winter.
When a cat decides to leave,
the deer in the woods look up,
awed by small creatures
that walk through the woods
as if they do not need protection.
When a cat decides to leave,
he knows the right direction.
He knows to walk past the birds
and the deer and the coyote,
far past the hole of a groundhog
that used to share his water,
into the woods where morels grow
and ferns and small violets
that bloom when sun falls
in early spring in small patches.
He knows to keep going and going.
When a cat decides to leave,
he does not need to take a thing.
He just goes the way of cats that go—
to that far place where cats go
after they are done with watching birds
and chasing squirrels and eating cat food
and playing with toys that roll.
When a cat decides to go,
there is nothing for us to do but wave.
Goodbye, cat, goodbye.

Suzanne Morris
A Blue Shroud
—*for McKenna (1999 – 2015)*

An old blue sheet,
from who knows where
or how long we'd had it;

faded, tearing at the hem,
ink-stained from morning entries
in my journal

and lines of poetry
composed with coffee
in bed;

draped to the floor at nights
to shield the bed skirt
from your earthy ways.

Of course I never ironed it.

But now you are gone.

Your rug is absent
from the foot of the bed
and you need not be
let out one more time
before turning off the light.

The blue sheet has become
your shroud; I helped to
wrap you in its dignity.

And though your absence
leaves the hem of my life
in shreds

oh, what comfort
in the days ahead,

knowing you are
tucked up tightly
in our commingled scents.

Suzanne Morris
Last Words of a Border Collie
— *for Boots*

What did you mean to say

when you heard the big truck
hurtling down the road that night?

What did you mean to say

when you crouched in its path,
ears peaked, eyes wide in alert?

What did you mean to say
as the head lights blinded you?

Danger ahead! Turn back now!

Rest easy, good fellow,
you were only trying to

do your job.

Your eyes were still wide open
when we found you.

Alice Campbell Romano
I Killed Our Dog

One lash of my tongue.
She came to comfort me.
I thought she wanted something
when I had nothing left.
Go away, Lena, go away and die.

Siberian girl in Los Angeles.
River runner, leash tugger,
blue eyes like sunlit ice.

My husband came home at night,
sat down, had long talks with you.
He howled things to you.
You howled things back.
I never had the knack.

The vet said it was kidney disease.
You would not get better
      & it would be best if we, etcetera,
      & when you would take
      nothing from us, not even water

My husband knelt by you
in the white room & hugged you.
      He cried, stroked you,
      & howled
      soft in your ear
      until you
      slumped.

"I Killed Our Dog" was previously published in *Mudfish* 21 (January 2020).

Ruth Sabath Rosenthal
Baby Talk

Our brood long-grown
on their own
precious doggie
to fill that emptiness
just weeks gone
speaking "baby"
so missed
the tenderness
it brought out in us
what should be
our golden years
not so golden
without her
without her
we find
ourselves
hard-pressed
to say anything
that lightens
conversation
the way she did

Phip Ross
A Lesson after De-Worming
— for Howie

In the backyard he smelled a shallow root
and burrowed and chewed it clean

and the wintering bulb plumbed
from the flower pot he gnawed

and brought to his kennel
like the corpse of a frozen rodent.

Even sooty sock rooted from the hamper
he ripped like road-side sinew.

These many holes and wounds in cloth and soil
mark a fathom of his animal wits and broken trials.

On this city block of poodle and puggle and woodle,
this raw and bony visitor is the odd bastard puppy of the ditch

bowed tonight at the bowl-full of kibbles
in the warm kitchen.

Still, it must never hurt to divine
beneath the ground your next meal

and show the human what he doesn't
think he needs to remember.

Phip Ross
Dogged

The slobber-swing
Was unimportant as the red tongue
Waggling in the maw
of tall-stained teeth.

You believed in your mucous-rimmed eyes
To move my hand to the door
To the biscuit bucket

To the window cracked
And the breeze that
Ladled scent to your flared nose.
To the trail on which I followed.

You were not my life's love
Dream come true.
A summer in Spain.

The shelter under your chin
Was where you drew
my fingers
Between your rusty jaw
To curl in winter
And remember.

Phip Ross
Fetch

I talked to my dog about my other dog
that died during a seizure. Howie.
Slick is not a good listener.
He doesn't want any part of the past.

Between his jowls, he jostles
the tennis ball to another side of his mouth
with a sloppy tongue and stares,
dangles the ball a bit further beyond
his molar grasp. He thinks he's teasing me:
Take it. Try it.
Slick flinches with every finger I uncurl.

Howie would jump on my lap
and drop his chin over my forearm.
Do you remember that, Slick?
I snatch the ball and fling it
to the other side of the yard
and wait for a different dog
to bring it back. Over and over
again.

Alice Sanford
Death and Resurrection

Most likely caught and ate a poisoned rat,
Our vet said. . . . My first dog. The golden one.
Maggots crawled from every orifice. For months
I thought they crawled in every family corpse,
Taking each body slowly back to rosebush earth.

My dreams dredged up our dead, sickenly sweet,
Looking for me, searching for all they'd loved.
No matter if I ran or hid, putrid bodies scuttled closer.
No matter if I tried to wake. I saw their shapes,
Malevolent as rats, like maggots, swarming.

But Granny said a body buried and boxed in steel,
Or more forgiving pine, waits 'til God's trumpets
Call and, then, in old corporeal form will rise.
Even if poisoned, she promised when I asked.

Lauren Scharhag
The Ledger

I have dealt with death before.
All my grandparents have passed away.
There was everything leading up to their passing,
then the mourning, which everyone knows
never really ends. It's just something you learn to carry.
Then I watched my parents go through all the practical hassles
of settling the estate: planning and paying for funerals,
insurance, probate, managing medical bills,
selling the houses, hauling furniture out to the curb.
A veritable slog of phone calls and paperwork.
Even now, eleven years after my grandmother died,
a life insurance policy we never knew she had
has surfaced, a small pay-out that has to be distributed.
But this is the first time I've had to do something
even remotely close to this.
The vet gave us a quote.
The appointment has been set.
Now, as I go over the monthly budget,
I realize I need to add a line item,
but I can't bring myself to write it in.
I will wait until afterwards.
I will label it with her name.

Lauren Scharhag
Jack & Lucy

I keep feeling soft thumps
on the edge of the bed at night.
Startled from sleep,
I raise my head and look
but you are not there.

I am still picking your fur
from the fibers of my clothes.
The towels in the laundry basket
retain the indent of your form.
Some of my books were mauled by you
in kittenhood, covers still dotted
with little tooth and claw marks,
a sort of feline Braille.

I touch them and recall
you pushing your head
into my palm.

Our time has made me--

I am loveless and adored.
I am empty and full.
I am lonely and never lonely.
I am joyless and overjoyed.

Karen Scott
Heaven?

When you lose a friend, surrender to the reality
of providing death with dignity,
you return in an empty car to an empty home.

Shortly afterwards you receive
paw prints in plaster
snips of hair
ashes in a wooden box with a golden plaque
and a copy of The Rainbow Bridge.

That's the scary part. A poem that promises
our departed, beloved pets wait for us, whole,
restored to health.

When we pass, we will meet them
in exuberant welcome and cross over
The Rainbow Bridge to Heaven, together.

OK, I don't know about you, but I have loved and cared for
many a pet in my lifetime so far. I shudder to think
that all of them are waiting for me to make an appearance.

My spiritual essence may be knocked
clean out of my corporeal body under the onslaught
of collies and Aussies, cats and parakeets.

Trampled by Boomer and Lassie, by Tank and Jessica,
Teacake, Midnight, Princess, and Tipper,
Niki and Nessie, Milo,
Pat and Parakeet Green Elizabeth Scott,
Assorted gerbils and hamsters
And even Charles, the frog I raised from a tadpole.

I may not be able to continue across to Heaven!

Karen Scott
Tadger at Sixteen

Feline senile dementia typically occurs after age fifteen.
— Dr. Katy Burr, DVM, Trupanion.com blog

Sometimes he comes to me
gazes with extra wide eyes
as if he doesn't remember who I am
gives an inquisitive meow.

Other times I walk into the kitchen,
see him studying the water bowl.
Not drinking
just staring.

Lately, fixated with the living room window,
he constantly surveys the bushes, the yard.
If I pull him off the window sill,
he scrabbles right back up.

If he wakes from a nap, finds himself alone,
he yowls. Such a heart-wrenching sound!
I'm in here I yell from the other room.
He quiets until he notices he is alone again.

Like that resident at every nursing home
and memory care unit I have visited
to see my grandmother
and now my mother.

Help me help me help me
echoes down the hall, across the dining room.
When someone asks what they need,
they keep up the litany

help me help me help me
often drowning out the words meant to comfort.
When Tadger yowls his confusion and
helplessness, I call out to reassure him

hoping that when it is my turn,
someone will call my name, saying
I am here.
What do you need?

Karen Scott
Transition
— for Tadger

A friend died in my arms today.
I was glad I was there
that I did not find his corpse upon returning home.

I had been his nurse for weeks, tending his wounds,
urging him to eat and drink.
I bundled his wasted frame, held him close,

his body already cooling, clear pool eyes
as cloudy as roller balls on Hadiya's perfume oils.
The interval between each breath lengthened

each exhalation a wheeze, a feeble utterance.
I told him *just let go.* I held him,
crooned soothingly, reminded him he was loved

How tenaciously we cling to life
long past the time we should just relinquish our grip
    and
        let
           go

Emily Simmons
Everything but the Horse

The new place needed fences strung before
horses could be brought with us. The pony
lays flat out as her fat, little legs rest
beside her, sunning in the mud. Today,
she's not stretched, limbs tucked under. I call her.

One leg unfurls, but the rest stay folded.
The mud sucks my boots each step out to her.
I kneel beside in the shit, soil and hay.
Muck encrusted in her coat from all the
times she rolled, while trying her best then to
put herself into the ground. Muzzle drawn
onto my lap, lift her lip to see pink
missing from her gums. Wet teeth marks along
her belly after trying to nip pain
out of her guts. I phone the vet to come.

A twenty-minute hospice of IV
xylazine begins as the children say
goodbye, and I stroke her neck as my hands
say farewell to the touch of her golden
mane, feeling warmth fade after her light flees
down the optic nerve; spirit evicted
by a needle to end the pain for her.

The body hauler recites his prayer and
pulls the blanket from her corpse, ropes wrapped tight
around her hooves as the winch starts. Chains click
as she rises up onto the bed, then
they drive away without me. Gravel marks
made by a dragged horse, my best friend of years
gone. I get in my car and leave the farm
to go home to everything but the horse.

Kashiana Singh
My Brother's Dog, Laika

for years I have
put its sound on a leash

Laika, your sparkling, slender
body
perfectly fitted into the
world.
Your nostrils quivered
in sleep, making others jealous
with how you got his attention
named so after the first mongrel
in space, Laika.

Laika, who joined the mission
to validate space
to prefix their story
while fulfilling a sad end
with a pounding heart.

you orbited him like
a prayer consistently
stable and kind.
he held you like
he was your earth.
your eyes
shimmering in sharp response
like darts to his deepening
sound —

Catch, he said
Go Catch
Laika

You were tonic to his youth
an unspoiled brat, like him
you too gazed into the eyes
of others with a sweetness

that crumbled their worlds.
I saw in you and him an
animated companionship
each time you gracefully
knocked at the door.

>   *racing*
>   *tumbling*
>   *folding*
>   *ears flapping*

nearly blind into his arms.
His days
glowed in your presence
your lives tucked into
each other
as if in knowledge
of what
was imminent
your pictures
bristle with friendship
simple moments
so expansive, you
staring at the camera
both breathless
it jolted me back —
It is raining today
I heard
you bark outside
lingering as you did
at the edge of his heels.
I nudge your scent away
Go, catch Laika, I say
It makes me want to ask though —

Are you both together, now?
Does he lean against you?

In his blue plaid shirt, his
cuffs unbuttoned
convenient

you at his side
quiet as you chew
so familiar, so present, so near
his hands reflexively
linger around your neck
ready for a quick walk.

Kashiana Singh, "My Brother's Dog Laila" *Woman by the Door,* Apprentice House Press 2022

Jess Skyleson
Looking Back

I remember the delighted way
you looked at me, waking up
and waiting
at the foot of the bed,
happy just to see my eyes
opening once again—

I remember the expectant way
you looked at me, hearing your name,
not knowing
what else I was saying, but content
to realize, somehow,
you were on my mind—

I remember the quiet way
you looked at me, when I was too sick
to move from the couch, and you,
worried,
could only lay your head
in my lap with tender concern—

I remember the disappointed way
you looked at me, when I would leave
each morning, heading off to places
where you could never follow,
and the instant forgiveness
in your eyes, each time I returned—

I hope you could see the love
in my own eyes, that day it was finally you,
leaving me, and I knew
it would be the last time
we would look
at each other.

Kristyn Snedden
Murphy's Requiem

The big black dog came to her, through
surprising events, some would say
he found her, and he was the closest
she would ever know to a wounded healer,
his purpose hidden deep within silky black fur.

His brown eyes watched her, and it took
some months before he willingly offered
his white belly for a rub.
The dog didn't know the path she was on
or see the troubles that had shattered her

into constellations seeking connection
and yet, he knew her call. They climbed the hill
that beckoned, slipping in Georgia clay,
and the dog, the big black dog,
stayed right beside her.

Kudzu covered the trellis
hiding the cave that cradled every memory -
the tender and the violent,
and all the lies between.
She began the excavation with his eyes, her witness.

Wet air pressed down on fungal growth.
Decades had passed in the dark, preparing
this place – this place
kept calling her, over and over,
speaking in tongues,

glossolalia, lalia, lalia.
Jet-black stalagmites, bejeweled stalactites,
floating helictites,
each with its own ghosts.
She thought she would feel sad,

and she watched for tears

but who was she fooling?
In that moment
there was only the dog
right there, beside her.

He still visits her in dreams.

Betty Stanton
Leaving Stones

I think he's the only Jew buried in Woodlawn, have spent years wandering between headstones - Memorial Day, Labor Day, Veteran's Day - his headstone the only one with the star etched just below his middle name, the only one where stones have been left to keep the soul down, bind him into *beit olam,* to wait for God. Every other grave has flowers, plastic that fades and withers and rots forgotten back into the earth.

> Stones last like memory.
> Stones do not rot. Do not die.

Last week King died. I missed the ringing of my phone six times in a row because I was teaching a lecture on theatrical lighting design, explaining that the oils on just the fingertips are enough to leave too much residue on the bulb, enough to shatter it into a thousand pieces. *We have to protect things that are fragile, that are worth something*, I told my students, and then I checked messages.

A lap dog who didn't know his own hundred and eighty pounds of flesh, when my father was handcuffed to cylinders of oxygen every minute of the day and couldn't take himself to the bathroom he made my mother promise that she'd take care of his dog. Now his ashes lie over his grave.

> We leave stones for them both.

Joseph Stanton
Cat

What can be said without cliché
regarding the bit of tabby
that so often leaned against me;
climbed into my lap;
purred as if to persuade me
I was something more than Mr. Food;
slept always on my bed,
ignoring the kids attempts
to make him sleep on theirs;
and offered so insistently
his monosyllabic pleas
in behalf of those cans of Friskies
so many of which still haunt the shelves,
weeks after Kenny has gone the way of all fur-balls?

I used to tell myself
I worried about a pet's demise
only for my kids' sake.
Stuff of legend in our family history
were the downfalls of Banana and Blueberry,
worried to death, no doubt,
by the coming of Kenny.

Blueberry fell first,
sending me, carcass in hand,
from pet store to pet store
while my daughter was in school,
searching for an exact match
of blue and green feathers.
Suzy was in her twenties before I finally explained
why Blueberry underwent the sudden personality shift,
from Jekyll to Hyde,
that led to Banana's distress.

With Kenny, too, I find myself
the bearer of all our griefs,
the children gone now to other cities,

their cat more a memory
to them of childhood
than the ornery critter,
the bane of my day to day,
who, it now seems,
it is so hard for me
to do without.

Best to end, I guess, with irony and Eliot,
remembering we committed to memory,
for Suzy's fifth-grade recitation,
"Macavity: The Mystery Cat,"
declaring in those long rides to school,
that there is no one like Macavity,
a cat of such deceitfulness and suavity,
who always has an alibi, and one or two to spare,
even when it seems, at last,
Macavity's not there.

Claire Taylor
September, Again

I sat in the wet grass
before dawn and fed you
by the spoonful like a child,
hoping for a healing that didn't come.

As they carried you away
I snipped black-eyed Susans, lay them
where the ground was still warm
and left them to wilt.

One year and then another until
it's September again
and the garden bursts golden,
everywhere black-eyed Susans
shining in the late afternoon sun.

I slip up and call the new dog by your name.
He doesn't even lift his head.

Ingrid L. Taylor
Haunting

Glass passes through him, comes out
sharpened on the other side,

scintillating wing of beetle
dropped too fast and too soon.

I wish for a haunting,
a black shuck to hound my days.

I get only this:
a groan
a sigh
a soft body stretched beneath the sun,

warm fur to hold between my fingers.

Ingrid L. Taylor
How Far We Could Run
— *for Trixie*

Your name conjured
from a cartoon,
edged in black & waiting
for your colors. Collared
to a home with more sorrow
than love. That first night
you cried into darkness, exiled
from the comfort of siblings,
to be bellowed into silence.
Together we learned
the secrets of sisterly love,
the pathologies of prayer,

& the rules of sudden violence.
Together we discovered
the limits
of our hands and paws.
How far we could run
with welted limbs & closed throats.
We rolled on our backs,
our soft bellies
turning to the sky, our bodies
one length on the carpet.
My sister

I have not forgotten
how to disguise the pink
of my abdomen. I've kept the bruise
nurtured in your memory,
no balm to soothe the rage
of roses & guilty ghosts.
I chase your absence

in hollow spaces.
I search every pothole,
trench, & gully

just to make sure
no one is trapped
inside.

Peter Taylor
Dog Reincarnate

A whimper in the night and I'm pulled awake.
Quick out of bed and into my robe,
lift his weight, well known after fourteen years,
careful of my back, careful down the stairs,
carefully his rear legs down and then the front.
Into my winter coat, socks and boots,
scarf, hat, gloves; find the leash and flashlight.
He hoists himself down the two steps he can just manage
and we're out.
The night is frigid, still.
My hands and feet nearly numb as I take in the stars
for the quarter-hour he takes to find
just the right snowy spot to do his business.

Three or four times each night he whimpers—
pain? or not wanting to mess the floor after all these years of
thoughtfulness?—
as Orion, with faithful Sirius and Procyon, moves nightly west.
In early January the Quadrantids peak:
In ten minutes I see more shooting stars than I ever would
if sleep were not so interrupted.

Then one late January morning I carry his weight once more
(I thought he would have stiffened, but not yet)
wrapped in his old blanket.
We drive through the snow to a nice man
who gives me a moment
before I drive back home.
There are no stars in the sky, that I can see.
The brilliant day lies long, ahead.

For eighteen months I sleep all night,
empty except for dreams.
Sometimes in the morning my pillow is damp.

But now once again there are whimpers, and I'm pulled awake.
She's already halfway down the stairs before
bounding back to see that I'm coming.

Slip on a robe, a pair of sneakers, find the old leash.
She scampers to the door and looks back, urging me on.
Out we go, three or four times a balmy night,
not wanting to have a piddle on the floor.

Three months of this so far
and I could use a good night's sleep.
But I'm studying the stars again.

Orion has journeyed far; Polaris remains true north.

Alarie Tennille
Sisters

They weren't that close as sisters
we thought.
A long illness, stinking
of diarrhea and trips to the vet
distanced the cats
we thought.

The dying one fought to live,
demanded laps and special food,
while her sister withdrew
into a closet. *She understands*
we thought.

Four months later, our sleep
is still clawed awake by howls.
She searches upstairs,
downstairs, under the bed
and in the closets, calling
"Sister? Sister? Sister?"

"Sisters" was first published in Tennille's chapbook, *Spiraling into Control*, The Lives You Touch Publications (2010).

Kerry Trautman
Dead Cats

I had nothing to say to my mother
when her latest cat died.
They are always dying, after all.

They always seemed to find our house,
to cautiously rub our legs,
to eat a bit, to stay,
despite torn window screens,
waving in breezes,
despite the small flap doors
designed for them to leave on a whim.

My mother never stapled flyers
to telephone poles,
or placed a classified ad,
Found: Cat,
preferring, I suppose,
to leave the decision to the cat itself,
like a woman refusing to
force her lover to leave his wife,
instead providing her back-door key,
quietly hoping for its click and the clunk
of suitcases on linoleum.

Over the years I had come to expect
two or four furred boarders to opt
to linger for any given month or year,
until death or disappearance
yanked them from my mother's life.
These animals whose sleeping habits
she knew by rote,
whose vet bills staggered,
whose fleas she futilely bombed,
whose bathing caused bleeding, gauze.
All the while she could not name,
if asked, three of my friends,
my favorite poet or ice cream.

In the muffled stillness of
a rainy afternoon,
I remember a grey cat leapt to my bed,
lay on my open book,
warmed by the reading lamp,
rolled to reveal his belly,
which I relented and petted,
whispering into the fur,
stupid cat, why do you stay here?

And now, my mother is shaken
by the loss of another cat,
a tan one with
perpetually-dirtied white paws,
who hid under beds.

She said she *buried him with the others,*
and I, suddenly horrified,
wondered where that mass grave was—
decades of cold cat bodies
underfoot where I jumped rope
or shrieked in the sprinkler,
or read, alone, in the shade of a maple.
Mom clenched her jaw
against approaching sobs,
and I said nothing,
turned my face to the grass.

"Dead Cats" was first published in *Nine Lives Later: A Dead Cat Anthology*, Dee Dee Chapman, ed. 2016.

Kerry Trautman
Stray III

When I scratch the head of my sister's Siamese
cat on her couch, I don't imagine how it might die. But these

three little kittens—slinking in through my glass
door to eat under the kitchen table—the idiocy

in loving their round eyes and point-tip tails, the stupid
heartbreak is how each time they slip through the glass, the big

bad world is waiting. One of my sister's cats lived eighteen
years, dozing at the end of her bed, never once sinking

a paw in snow. As a girl, I remember petting the oily
fur of our fifteen-year-old cat who stopped washing,

her eyes glazed like a broken spell. But I know what
happens to soft things left outside. Like the Thumbelina

doll I lost playing Neverland in July marigolds, found
next March, dress sun-bleached gray, rubbery face split brow

to chin. I bring it on myself each time. I bite the apple,
don't I? Touch my finger-pad to the spindle,

falling in love with more things than I am able
rescue. The least I could do is stop guessing their names.

Mark Tulin
A Tonkinese Pedigree

Rudy was a mixture
of Siamese and Burmese—
a Tonkinese cat with a pedigree

A breed unto his own,
he walked on tiptoes with head held high,
while the other cats were fickle
and failed to groom

Rudy made his residence by the window,
and drew boundaries
that tabbies refused to cross

A moody feline
with a hiss and roar,
whom others called eccentric,
rarely used his scratchpad
or chase a fake mouse down the hall

Some cats have no legacy,
but Rudy was an Egyptian deity,
buried with the Pharaohs.

Mark Tulin
Remnants of You

His treats in the cupboard,
his bowl of water half full—
at the edge of the sofa,
he frayed the fabric with his claws

The cat carrier is still in storage,
along with his toys
and his catnip ball

His spot by the window is vacant—
no more teeth-chattering at birds
or imagining himself chasing squirrels—

Still some clumps of fur
left on his favorite chair,
a litter tray in the basement
with a scooper on the shelf

The remnants of you remain—
your paws on my belly,
making bread.

Alan Walowitz
Ghost-Cat

Cats seldom take the time to settle their affairs.
Finances aren't put in place,
letters from former lovers burned,
too many cans half-eaten
that might have given comfort to those
who just happen by.

Same as us all, I believe in ghosts
and there are noises in an old house
that can't be explained away,
the pipes screwed in backwards from the day they were laid,
or the boiler needs to be cleaned again--
till nothing is left of its insides, like an ulcer,
the earnest and dyspeptic plumber replies
as he hands over the bill.
Each night I hear footsteps on the attic stairs,
though the attic's been sealed
long as we've been here.
Sometimes those steps are heavy and human,
but what do I care?
Those restless spirits need a place.

But sometimes they're soft and might be Chocky,
attending to things at last--
though I never want him to feel obliged.
Shit happens, as his missing the litterbox
often his last few years will attest.
Though he liked to complain,
he seemed happy enough,
except when we were tardy
opening one last can.
Or were too slow to jiggle the tap
just a quarter-turn more.
Then, I hear a voice say:
Chocolate, where are you?
It's my daughter.
Or, *I thought he'd be in the tub waiting:*

My wife.
Or, *Kitten, if you're not here, where the hell did you go?*
That's me, talking to myself.
We like to talk to ourselves around here
and not any old, useless: *Come kitty, kitty.*
Or that sibilant hiss that's not anything at all
even a ghost-cat would bear.

Instead, it's Chocky who'll say:
I've come to tie up some loose ends,
as he reaches for a ball of yarn,
he had hidden once behind the sofa
waiting for just the right occasion.
Though he'll soon become bored
and fall asleep right here where we're waiting,
or perhaps on the landing of the make-believe attic stairs--
the lonely prairie where he can make a bed
and the sun is warm and streaming in.

"Ghost-Cat" first appeared in *Verse-Virtual: An Online Community Journal of Poetry*, February, 2022.

Amy Sage Webb-Baza
Feet

No one prepares you
for a dog's feet, for the way
you'll rub your thumb
over those pads, or the way
you'll work to earn enough
trust for the dog to offer up
a limp wrist to let you clip
the nails. No one prepares you
for the time you'll spend
washing and drying those
feet, the way you'll dig
dried mud from the fuzz
between the toes, or
for the way a dog
reaches up when it wants
something, and touches
your leg with one paw.
Nothing prepares you
for the fact those feet
have a smell you'll miss
or for the way, after
a dog is gone, you listen
for the sound of those
feet on the stairs and the
click of those nails
approaching on the tile
every evening
to welcome you home.

Kathleen Weed
Absence (For Flora)

The shape of absence is a rectangle.
A rectangle no longer covered by
a spill-proof mat. A forsaken spot in
a corner of my kitchen where the heart
pine floor still looks shiny and new.

The taste of absence is a fry pan
of scrambled eggs that you licked
clean on the day the doctor knocked
at our front door, wearing her
kind face and hiding a big syringe.

The smell of absence is ghost
dander on a small blanket at the end
of my bed. Perfume of your shed cells
that, even as I bury my face in baby
blue wool, can no longer make me sneeze.

The sound of absence is someone
else's dog yapping at a hapless huckster
from behind her master's gate, or shaking
her own person's outstretched hand, with
a furry brown paw—somebody saying

Good dog.

Laura Grace Weldon
Open Like Hands
After "In Answer to Amy's Question What's a Pickerel"

I am reading a Plumly poem about pickerel.
It clicks open a lock in me, unrelated to
blue-black lakes or glass-eyed fish.
Electric-charged tears prickle my
eyes. For reasons only poetry
knows it summons our dog
Winston, fierce acolyte of
a religion devoted to
perpetual affection.
If a fish poem can
bring him back
from the dead,
what might a
poem do
for you?

"Open Like Hands" was previously published in *Portals* (Middle Creek, 2021).

Laura Grace Weldon
This German Shepherd

Who he was lingers with us,
his fear of water, love of cats,
his tail swish, glad sniff,
tired *garumphf* at the day's close.

In his thirteenth year, this good dog
walked with me despite
the disease that would take him.
One bright day he yanked me into a ditch
as a truck hurtled past.
The driver braked hard, backed up, blamed
sun in his eyes, said the dog saved me.

I know there are greater sorrows,
still, a shock of grief shook loose
when Jedi Moon had to be put down.

While reading on the couch,
I sometimes let one hand dangle
to rest on the memory of his vigilant spine.

Previously published in *Blackbird* (Grayson Books, 2019)

Jon Wesick
Stay

"I don't know if I can stay with Ron." Kim secured a lock of hair behind her ear. "You know? When his dog Abby died, he took her to a taxidermist and had her stuffed."

"No!" Donna dropped some crumbs onto the patio for the sparrows.

"Don't believe me? I'll show you," Kim said.

I drained my Anhui Silver Sprout tea and walked down the wooden stairs so a barista could pour more hot water over the leaves. By the time I returned, the women had decided we'd drive in separate cars. Donna and I followed Kim's Toyota Corolla into a subdivision of identical condos with beige stucco walls and tile roofs. Kim parked, led us up the stairs, and unlocked Ron's front door. The interior was clean and neat with a bowl of apples and bananas on the glass, dining table. We followed Kim into their bedroom where she slid open a mirrored door to reveal the stuffed golden retriever lying with chin on paw atop a cushion in a wicker doggy bed.

"See what I mean!" Kim paced back and forth.
Abby wasn't creepy. She was simply missing something like a plastic flower or a butterfly sample impaled on a pin. Donna and Kim went to pack. Before leaving, I turned for one last look at Abby and said, "Stay."

Fred Zirm
First Walk without My Dog

I follow in her footsteps
where once she followed
mine – or rather where
we once walked together:
me, intent on exercise,
she, on exploration.

Too late, I realize
all dogs are guide dogs,
alerting us to what we
might miss, all the unseen
mysteries of place and time
in a twig or leaf or clump
of grass that tell us where
we are and who's been here before.

At the end, she refused to eat
what she could not process,
just as I cannot digest her death
and deny it still: checking
her water dish, leaving
her leash hanging by
the front door, and looking
for her to come to me
even now, as I call.

My senses are not as keen
as hers, though her absence
has sharpened them some.
I pause to sniff the breeze
she knew so much better than I
and try to read the world
as she did – alive, alive, alive.

Fred Zirm
Undiscovered Country

One-by-one, my dogs have run ahead
as scouts to sniff out our mortality.
They've shown me how to grow
grey and stiff and deaf - and doze all day.
As pups, they took pride in giving me
the sticks they scampered to retrieve,
while I took joy in their returning,
but once they staggered into a deeper sleep,
they could bring nothing back to save me
from the twitch and whimper of my own dreams
or the darkness of that final fetching.

"Undiscovered Country" was published, previously, in *Neat*. (March, 2015.)

Contributor Bios

Sandra Anfang is a Northern California poet, teacher, and editor. Her poems have been published in numerous print and online journals including *Rattle*, *The New Verse News*, *The MacGuffin*, and *Spillway*. Her poetry collections include *Looking Glass Heart* (Finishing Line Press, 2016), *Road Worrier: Poems of the Inner and Outer Landscape* (Finishing Line Press, 2018), and *Xylem Highway* (Main Street Rag, 2019). She has been nominated for a Best Short Fictions award, Best of the Net, and a Pushcart Prize. She recently earned second and third place prizes in the Prose Poem division of the Soul-Making Keats contest and second place in the San Francisco International Haiku contest. Anfang is founder and host of the monthly series, Rivertown Poets (established 2013), and a poetry teacher in the public schools. Samples of her poetry and visual art can be seen at sandeanfangart.com.

Catherine Arra is a former high school English and writing teacher. Her poetry and prose have appeared in numerous literary journals online and in print, and in several anthologies. She is the author of *Solitude, Tarot & the Corona Blues* (Kelsay Books, 2022), *Deer Love* (Dos Madres Press, 2021), *Her Landscape, Poems Based on the Life of Mileva Marić Einstein* (Finishing Line Press, 2020), (*Women in Parentheses*) (Kelsay Books, 2019), *Writing in the Ether* (Dos Madres Press, 2018), and three chapbooks. Arra lives in upstate New York where she teaches part-time and facilitates local writing groups. Find her at www.catherinearra.com

Madeline Artenberg was a photojournalist and street theatre performer before falling for poetry. After the first poem popped out, she sold all her cameras. She has become a well-known performance poet in the NYC area. Her work appears in publications, such as *Rattle*, *The Poet*, *Literature Today International Journal*, and *MacQueens Quinterly*. She was semi-finalist in *Margie, The American Journal of Poetry* contest, and finalist in *Mudfish* 2020 contest. One of her poems was nominated as *Best of the Net* 2020 by *Poets Wear Prada*.

Lucinda Atkins has published in *Stone Poetry Journal* and *Trouvaille Review*.

Lana Hechtman Ayers has shepherded over one hundred poetry volumes into print in her role as managing editor for three small presses. Her work appears in print and online in places such as *Rattle, Snake Nation Review,* and *Verse Daily,* as well as in her eleven collections. Visit her online at http://LanaAyers.com

Tina Barry is the author of *Beautiful Raft* (Big Table Publishing, 2019), and *Mall Flower* (Big Table Publishing, 2016). Her poems and fiction have appeared in numerous literary publications such as *Rattle, The Best Small Fictions 2020* (spotlighted story) and *2016, Drunken Boat, The American Poetry Journal, Lascaux Review, Sky Island Journal, Nasty Women Poets,* and *A Constellation of Kisses*. Tina is a three-time Pushcart Prize nominee and has several Best of the Net nods. She is a teaching artist at The Poetry Barn and Writers.com.

Rachel R. Baum is a former librarian, professional dog trainer, licensed private pilot, and kayak angler. Her poems have appeared in *Raven'sPerch, High Shelf Press, Wingless Dreamer, Poetica Review, Bark magazine, Around the World anthology* and others. She is author of the blog *BARK! Confessions of a Dog Trainer*, and editor of *Funeral and Memorial Service Readings Poems and Tributes* (McFarland, 1999).

Ruth Bavetta's poems have appeared in *Rattle, Nimrod, Tar River Poetry, North American Review, Slant, American Journal of Poetry,* and many other journals and anthologies. Her fifth book is *What's Left Over*, FutureCycle Press, 2022. She has been an Associate Editor for *Good Works Review* and has been nominated for Best of the Net and the Pushcart Prize. She likes the light on November afternoons, the music of Stravinsky, and the smell of the ocean. She hates pretense, fundamentalism, and sauerkraut.

Shelly Blankman lives in Columbia, Maryland, with her husband of 40 years, three rescue cats, and a foster dog. They have two sons, Richard and Joshua, who reside in New York and Texas, respectively. Shelly's educational and career paths have followed public relations and journalism, but her first love has always been poetry. Her work has been published in such publications as *New Verse News, Halfway Down The Stairs*, and *The Ekphrastic Review*. Richard and Joshua recently published her first book of poetry, *Pumpkinhead*.

Eric Chiles began teaching Writing and Journalism at colleges in eastern Pennsylvania after a career in newspapers. He is the author of the chapbook *Caught in Between*, and his poetry has appeared in such journals as *The American Journal of Poetry*, *Canary*, *Chiron Review*, *Main Street Rag*, *Rattle*, *San Pedro River review*, *Tar River Poetry*, and elsewhere.

Rick Christiansen is a former corporate executive, stand-up comedian, actor and director. His work is published or forthcoming in *Oddball Magazine*, *Muddy River Poetry Review*, *Stone Poetry Journal*, *The Raven's Perch*, *The Rye Whiskey Review*, *As It Ought to Be Magazine*, *WINK Magazine*, and other journals and magazines. He is the co-host of SpoFest and a member of The St. Louis Writers Guild. He lives in Missouri near his eight grandchildren.

Jane Connelly is an artist and writer who lived in Guam, M.I., before moving to Long Island, NY. She has won numerous awards and has been published in *The Avocet*, *The Bard's Review*, *Nassau County Poet Laureate Society Review*, *Oberon*, and *Performance Poets Anthology*, and most recently in the Walt Whitman Birthplace Association's Anthology "Covid". She is on the Advisory Committee of the Nassau County Poet Laureate Society, and a member of "SIP"/Sisters in Poetry.

Lynda V. E. Crawford has lived in the US longer than her childhood home Barbados. Both homes sway and punctuate her writing. Lynda writes to sneak behind eyes, blow through ears, stretch voices like others dance words. She's been a journalist, copywriter, website manager, and email marketer. Poetry won't let go. Her work has appeared or is forthcoming in various journals and anthologies including *The Caribbean Writer*, *The Galway Review*, *The Bookends Review* and *Exposition Review*.

Megan Dausch is a writer and accessibility specialist from New York. She makes her home with her husband and guide dog. Her work has appeared in *Claw & Blossom*, *Bards Annual 2021*, *Third Wednesday*, and *The Tishman Review*.

Dave Day is an attorney from Honolulu, Hawaii, who was the owner of Darwin, the Australian Cattle Dog. He has published poetry in *The Ekphrastic Review* and *The New Verse News* and extremely non-poetic articles in the *Emory International Law Review* and the *Hawaii Bar Journal*.

Robert L. Dean, Jr. is the author of *The Aerialist Will not be Performing*: *ekphrastic poems and flash fictions to the art of Steven Schroeder* (Turning Plow Press, 2020), *At the Lake with Heisenberg* (Spartan Press, 2018), and his recent chapbook, *Pulp* (Finishing Line Press, 2022). A multiple Best of the Net nominee and a Pushcart nominee, his work has appeared in many publications. He has been a professional musician and worked at The Dallas Morning News. He lives Augusta, Kansas.

Jane Desmond is a poet who lives in Illinois and writes often about animals and the more-than-human world. Her work has appeared in *The Shrew Literary Journa*l; *Persimmon Tree*; *Words for the Wild* (U.K.); and the *Mason Street Literary Review*, among other places. As a scholar who specializes in human-animal studies, she serves on both the anthropology and veterinary college faculties at the University of Illinois at Urbana-Champaign.

Shane Dickie is a Canadian poet who graduated from Crandall University with a B. A. in English. He worked at the Times-Transcript and performed in live theatre. His hobbies include swimming, bee-keeping, walking in the woods, spying for mushrooms, and bird watching for woodpeckers.

Linda Trott Dickman is an award-winning poet, and author of four chapbooks. Her work has been featured in local, international, and online anthologies. She is the coordinator of poetry for the Northport Arts Coalition. She teaches at local museums and leads a poetry workshop at Samantha's Li'l Bit O' Heaven coffee house.

Sara Kass Eifler is a queer vegan Jewish woman with an abiding interest in poetry, folklore, and sacred story. She lives on the traditional territory of the Wôpanâak (Wampanoag) and Nauset nations on Cape Cod with her partner. Her creative work is published or forthcoming in journals such as *Green House* and *iō Literary*. Follow her on Twitter: @sarakasseifler.

Mary Belardi Erickson lives in west central Minnesota with her husband, Jon; cat, Valentine; and Lhasa apso mix, Georgene. She has always been close to her pets and likes writing about them, especially humorous poems about their antics. When one passes, she finds a need to write poetry as part of her grieving process and the wish to remember them. Mary Belardi Erickson has published the last couple decades online and in print. She has two chapbooks: *While You Blue-step*, by Aldrich Press, and *Barn Climbing*, about growing up on the prairie in Southern Minnesota.

R. Gerry Fabian is a poet and novelist. He has published four books of his published poems, *Parallels, Coming Out Of The Atlantic, Electronic Forecasts* and *Ball On The Mound.*
Twitter @GerryFabian2. Linkedin https://www.linkedin.com/in/gerry-fabian-91353a131/
Facebook https://www.facebook.com/profile.php?id=100010099476497

Lee Eric Freedman is the 3rd Poet Laureate of Swampscott, Massachusetts (2016-2018). Since 2011 he's been affectionately entitled as the Renegade Poet Laureate of Swampscott (2011-FOREVER) (This honorarium bestowed upon him by his friend and storyteller Tony Toledo). He is truly honored and humbled to be both. When Lee isn't busy being any type of Laureate he leads the Tin Box Poets of Swampscott Workshop Group, hosts the monthly First Friday Open Mic @ ReachArts Swampscott and regularly performs at open-mics all over the place. He is a three-time winner of the Naomi Cherkofsky Memorial Poetry Contest. Lee resides in Swampscott, Massachusetts. "end" (1988), about the death of his dog Happie, is the fourth poem he ever wrote.

Linda McCauley Freeman is the author of the full-length poetry collection *The Family Plot* (Backroom Window Press, 2022) and has been widely published in international journals, including in a Chinese translation. She was nominated for a Pushcart Prize 2022. Recently, she appeared in *Delta Poetry Review, Poet Magazine, Amsterdam Quarterly*, and won Grand Prize in StoriArts' Maya Angelou poetry contest. She received a grant from Arts MidHudson and was selected for Poets Respond to Art 2020, 2021 and 2022 shows. She was a three-time winner in the Talespinners Short Story contest judged by Michael Korda. She has an MFA from Bennington College and is the former poet-in-residence of the Putnam Arts Council. She lives in the Hudson Valley, NY. Follow her at www.Facebook.com/LindaMcCauleyFreeman

Audrey Friedman is a retired Rhode Island Literacy teacher who now lives an artsy life in Bluffton, SC. She writes poetry, paints, spins and knits. Audrey received her MFA in Poetry from Vermont College of the Fine Arts in 2005 and attending the renowned Bread Loaf Writers' Conference. She served as contributing editor for the *Hunger Mountain Literary Journal.* Audrey's work appears in journals including *The Comstock Review, California Quarterly, The Griffin, McQueen's Quinterly,* and *Stone Poetry Journal.*

Charlotte M. Friedman received her MFA from Vermont College of Fine Arts and her MS in Narrative Medicine from Columbia University, where she taught in the English Department for ten years. Her book, *The Girl Pages* was published by Hyperion, and her poems in journals such as *Connecticut River Review, Intima,* and *Waterwheel Review.* "Alams for Cleaning Out the Painter's House" was recently nominated for a Pushcart Prize and Best of the Net. Her poetry translations (with Carol Rose Little) have been published in *Latin American Literature Today* and *World Literature Today.*

Marianne Gambaro's poems have been published in print and online journals including *Mudfish, CALYX, Oberon Poetry Magazine, Pirene's Fountain,* and *The Naugatuck River Review.* Her chapbook, *Do NOT Stop for Hitchhikers,* was published by Finishing Line Press. Her career as a journalist is often reflected in the narrative style of her poetry. She is a member of the Florence (MA) Poets Society and serves on the editorial team for *Silkworm,* their annual journal. She lives, writes, and gardens in verdant Western Massachusetts, with her photographer-husband and two feline muses. She also does cat enrichment at her regional humane society. https://margampoetry.wordpress.com/

Roberta Gould's work has appeared widely in poetry journals and anthologies, including *Confrontation, Mid American Review, Green Mountain,* and *The Art and Craft of Poetry.* Her thirteen books, include *Woven Lightning* (Spuyten Duyvil Press), *Talk When You Can Tell the Truth* (2020), *Not By Blood Alone, Dream Yourself Flying* (Four Zoas Press), and *In Houses With Ladders* (Waterside Press). In Mexico, she organized an educational campaign for international tourists and their dealings with service people. She has translated poetry of Sor Juana, Jorge Luis Borges, and major poets writing in Spanish. She lives in the Hudson Valley. robertagould.net

Lola Haskins' most recent collection of poems — *Asylum: Improvisations on John Clare* (University of Pittsburgh Press, 2019) — was featured in the NY Times Sunday Magazine. Past honors include the Iowa Poetry Prize, two NEAs, two Florida Book Awards, narrative poetry prizes from *Southern Poetry Review* and *New England Poetry Review*, a Florida's Eden prize for environmental writing, and the Emily Dickinson *Writer Magazine* Award from Poetry Society of America. She serves as Honorary Chancellor of the Florida State Poets Association.

Vali Hawkins-Mitchell works and writes from her office across the street from the Honolulu Zoo. She is a Disaster and Trauma specialist and an award-winning artist. Her books, poetry, non-fiction, and creative fiction have been published in numerous literary and professional trade journals, such as *Sky Island Journal, Star82Review, Blink-ink*, and *The Disaster Recovery Journal*. For more information about Dr. Vali's art and writing, go to her website at www.valihawkinsmitchell.com

Damian Ward Hey is published in, among other places, *The RavensPerch, Trouvaille Review, e·ratio, Neologism, Trailer Park Quarterly*, and *The Rye Whiskey Review*. His poems appear in the anthologies: *Birth - Lifespan Vol. 1.* (Pure Slush); *Poets with Masks On* (Melanie Simms, ed.); and *easing the edges: a collection of everyday miracles* (d. ellis phelps, ed.). Hey has a BA in English from Columbia University and a Ph.D. in Comparative Literature from Stony Brook University. He is a professor of English at Molloy University and is the founding editor of *Stone Poetry Quarterly* (formerly *Stone Poetry Journal*). stonepoetryjournal.com.

Patricia Hope's award-winning writing has appeared in *Chicken Soup for the Soul, Number One, Pigeon Parade Quarterly, 2021 Anthology of Appalachian Writers, The Mildred Haun Review, Liquid Imagination, American Diversity Report,* and many others. She lives in Oak Ridge, Tennessee.

Lydia Horvath is a long-time Old West End Toledo resident and art teacher at Toledo School for the Arts. She is a mixed media artist and printmaker and does caricatures as a side gig. She sings in a cover band and a choir, as well as in her car. Writing is a newer pursuit for her, spanning the past four years or so. She's placed in the TMA Ekphrastic contest once, and the Ode to the Zip Code a couple of times. She has had work published in *Khroma* and *Pangolin Review*. Don't get her started about Modernist architecture or typography.

Amy Karon's poems have appeared or are forthcoming in *Cricket Magazine, PANK, Kahini, deLuge, Claw and Blossom, Eastern Iowa Review, Lagan Online, Half Mystic Journal*, and *Eternal Haunted Summer*. She is a freelance writer in rural Washington.

A New Englander with old farming roots, **Karen Kilcup**, is the Elizabeth Rosenthal Excellence Professor of English, Environmental & Sustainability Studies, and Women's, Gender, & Sexuality Studies at UNC Greensboro. Her book, *The Art of Restoration*, was awarded the 2021 Winter Goose Poetry Prize and will be published later this year. An avid cook, runner, and rock climber, she's always trying to resist the urge for More Garden.

Laurie Kolp is an avid runner and lover of nature living in southeast Texas with her husband, three children, and two dogs. She is the author of *Upon the Blue Couch* and *Hello, It's Your Mother*. Her poems have appeared in *San Pedro River Review, SWWIM, Rust + Moth*, and more.

Rick Lupert has been involved with poetry since 1990. A Pushcart Prize and Best of the Net nominee, he created PoetrySuperHighway.com and hosts the weekly Virtual Cobalt Cafe series. His twenty-six collections of poetry, include *God Wrestler*, and *I Am Not Writing a Book of Poems in Hawaii*. He edited the anthologies, *A Poet's Siddur, A Poet's Haggadah, The Night Goes on All Night*, and *Ekphrastia Gone Wild*. He works as a music teacher and graphic designer in Newhall, California.

Bernadette Martonik lives in Seattle, Washington. Her work can be found in *Oddball Magazine, Cathexis Northwest Press, Pithead Chapel, The Manifest-Station, The Extraordinary Project, Typishly, Vox Lux Journal,* and *Stone Pacific Zine*. She can be found on Twitter and Instagram @BernadetteMarto

Glen A. Mazis taught philosophy for decades at Penn State Harrisburg, retiring in 2020. He has more than 90 poems in literary journals, including *Rosebud, The North American Review, Sou'wester, Spoon River Poetry Review, Willow Review, Atlanta Review, Reed Magazine* and *Asheville Poetry Review*, and the collection, *The River Bends in Time* (Anaphora Literary Press, 2012), a chapbook, *The Body Is a Dancing Star* (Orchard Street Press, 2020), and another collection, *Bodies of Space and Time* is in press with Kelsay Books. He has published five philosophy books with the most recent being, *Merleau-Ponty and the Face of the World: Silence, Ethics, Imagination and Poetic Ontology* (SUNY Press). He is the 2019 winner of the Malovrh-Fenlon Poetry Prize (Orchard Street national contest).

Joan Mazza worked as a medical microbiologist, psychotherapist, and taught workshops on understanding dreams and nightmares. She is the author of six self-help psychology books, including *Dreaming Your Real Self*. Her poetry has appeared in *Crab Orchard Review, Valparaiso Poetry Review, Prairie Schooner, Adanna Literary Journal, Slant, Poet Lore,* and *The Nation*. She lives in rural central Virginia.

Shallene McGrath, a retired legal secretary, is one of the co-founders of Garden Valley Writer's Group. Her poetry has been published in *Stink Eye Magazine, Stone Poetry Journal, Sacramento News & Review,* and *Poetry Now*. She has read at numerous featured readings in Sacramento, New Orleans, and the greater San Francisco Bay Area. By invitation, she has read her poetry at high schools and Sacramento State University. She has run readings in Sacramento, CA, and New Orleans, LA. She resides in Garden Valley, Idaho, with her husband and cat, where she actively participates in the local art and writing community.

Robin Michel's poetry and prose have appeared in *Blue Mountain Review, Comstock Review, Lindenwood Review, The MacGuffin, Northampton Poetry Review, Rappahannock Review, San Pedro River Review, Saturday Evening Post, Switchgrass Review*, and elsewhere. Editor of *How to Begin: Poems, Prompts, Tips and Writing Exercises from the Fresh Ink Poetry Collective* (Raven & Wren Press, 2020), Robin has a master's degree in educational leadership and is a communications consultant for nonprofits and educational institutions.

She lives in San Francisco. You can find her at www.robinmichelwriter.com or on Instagram: @robinlmichel.

Felicia Mitchell makes her home in the mountains of Virginia, where she taught English and creative writing for 33 years at Emory & Henry College. Her poems appear in a range of publications, including in the recent anthology *Mountains Piled upon Mountains: Appalachian Nature Writing in the Anthropocene* (edited by Jessica Cory for WVU Press). *Waltzing with Horses*, a collection of poems, is available from Press 53. *A Mother Speaks, A Daughter Listens* is her most recent book. Website: www.feliciamitchell.net

For forty years, **Suzanne Morris** was a novelist, with eight published works beginning with *Galveston* (Doubleday, 1976) and most recently *Aftermath - a novel of the New London school tragedy, 1937* (SFASU Press, 2016). Often her poetry was attributed to characters in her fiction. Nowadays she devotes all her creative energies to writing poems. Her work is included in the anthologies, *No Season for Silence - Texas Poets and Pandemic* (Kallisto GAIA Press, 2020), and *Lone Star Poetry* (Kallisto GAIA Press, 2022). Her poems have appeared in *The Texas Poetry Assignment* and *The New Verse News*. www.suzannepagemorris.com

Maria Nazos is a Greek-American poet who was raised in Athens. Kaveh Akbar chose her work as one of the 2022 Palette Poetry Contest winners. Her poetry, translations, and essays are published in *The New Yorker, Cherry Tree, Birmingham Review, North American Review, Denver Quarterly,* and *Mid-American Review*. She is the author of *A Hymn That Meanders* (2011 Wising Up Press) and the chapbook *Still Life* (2016 Dancing Girl Press). Maria has received scholarships and fellowships from the Sewanee Writers' Conference, the University of Nebraska, where she took her PhD in Creative Writing, and the Vermont Studio Center. She lives with two crazy cats and a patient husband in Lincoln, Nebraska. You can find her at www.marianazos.com.

Alice Campbell Romano is a New Yorker who spent more than a decade in Italy, adapting Italian movie scripts into English. Her work appears in print journals and online, most recently or forthcoming in *Willows Wept Review; Ekphrastic Review's Starry Starry Night Anthology; Prometheus Dreaming; NewVerse News; Beyond Words,*

Instant Noodles; Orchards Poetry Journal; Snapdragon Journal; and *New Croton Review*. Alice and her dashing, Italian, filmmaking husband want a new canine partner, but they travel, including visits to grandchildren whose four-legged housemates Alice considers grandchildren, too.

Ruth Sabath Rosenthal is well-published in the U.S. and internationally. In October 2006, her poem, "on yet another birthday," was nominated for a Pushcart Prize by Ibbetson Street Press. Ruth has authored a chapbook, *Facing Home*, published by Finishing Line Press and, also, five full-length poetry books published by Paragon Poetry Press, Inc.: *Of My Labor; Facing Home and beyond; little, but by no means small; Food: Nature vs Nurture*; and *Gone, But Not Easily Forgotten*. Additionally, Ruth edited the autobiography, *Manfred: His Story of Survival… from Concentration Camp to Freedom in America*. https://newyorkcitypoet.com

Phip Ross teaches in a community college, volunteers for community radio and in the county jail. His poetry has been accepted by lovers on an airplane as well as convenience store cashiers and café waitresses. He lives in Nebraska.

Alice Sanford lives in Nashville, Tennessee. She is a Vanderbilt graduate, affiliated with The Porch Collective, Rockvale Writers, Hudson Valley Writers, and Chattanooga Writers Guild. *ART/LIFE, Stone Poetry Journal*, and other print and on-line journals have published her work. When not teaching or writing, she pays attention to her city-yard's wildlife — birds, foxes, rabbits, coyotes, and grandchildren — or reads another good book.

Lauren Scharhag (she/her) is an associate editor for *GLEAM: Journal of the Cadralor*, and the author of thirteen books, including *Requiem for a Robot Dog* (Cajun Mutt Press) and *Languages, First and Last* (Cyberwit Press). She has had over 200 publications in literary venues around the world. Recent honors include the Stephen A. DiBiase Poetry Contest Award (finalist) and the Seamus Burns Creative Writing Prize. She has also been nominated for multiple Best of the Net, Pushcart Prize, and Rhysling Awards. She lives in Kansas City, MO. To learn more about her work, visit: www.laurenscharhag.blogspot.com

Karen Scott, a poet in Columbus, Ohio, is a member and ardent supporter of Ohio Poetry Association (OPA), a past participant in the Women of Appalachia Project and a proud member of the SALON writing group. Some of her work has been published in *Common Threads* [OPA anthology, 2013, 2016, 2018,2020, 2021], *She Speaks* [Women of Appalachia anthology, 2017, 2019, 2020], *Delirious: A Poetic Celebration of Prince* (2016), *Northern Appalachia Review* (2020), and the *Quarantine Zine* published by OPAWL. Another poem was made into a broadside that can be found on https://poetrysuperhighway.com.

Emily Simmons lives near Ann Arbor, Michigan on a horse farm with a husband, two children, and a ridiculous number of animals.

Kashiana Singh (http://www.kashianasingh.com/) calls herself a work practitioner and embodies the essence of her TEDx talk - Work as Worship into her everyday. Her chapbook *Crushed Anthills* from Yavanika Press in 2020 is a journey that unravels memory through 10 cities. She proudly serves as a Managing Editor for Poets Reading the News and her voice be read and heard on various international platforms. Kashiana's first poetry collection is called *Shelling Peanuts and Stringing Words*. Her newest full-length collection, *Woman by the Door* has just been released with Apprentice House Press.

Jess Skyleson (they/them) is a queer, autistic poet and former aerospace engineer who began writing after being diagnosed with stage IV cancer at age 39. Currently in remission, they're now exploring new worlds in creative writing, with particular interests in Narrative Medicine, computational and sound poetry, and early Zen Buddhist poems. They were awarded the 2022 Hippocrates Open Poetry and Medicine Prize, an Honorable Mention in the Tor House Poetry Prize and were a finalist for the Yemassee Poetry Prize and Kalanithi Writing Award. Their work has appeared in *Oberon Poetry Magazine*, *Nixes Mate Review*, *Months to Years*, and *Evocations*, among others, as well as in anthologies from Stillhouse Press, Renard Press, and Fly on the Wall Press.

Kristy Snedden has been a trauma psychotherapist for thirty-plus years. She began writing poetry in June 2020. Her work appears or is forthcoming in *Amethyst Review, Book of Matches, Poetry Super Highway, As Above, So Below, Door Is A Jar, Snapdragon,* and *Green*

Ink Poetry. She is currently a student at Phillip Schultz's The Writer's Studio. Reading and writing poetry is how she stays alive and engaged with a turbulent world. In her free time, she can be found hiking in the Appalachian Mountains near her home, soaking it in.

Betty Stanton (she/her) is a writer who lives and works in Tulsa, Oklahoma. Her work has appeared or is forthcoming in various journals and collections and has been included in anthologies from Dos Gatos Press and Picaroon Poetry Press. She received her MFA from The University of Texas - El Paso. twitter @ bfstanton http://bettystanton.weebly.com/

Joseph Stanton's seven books of poems are *Prevailing Winds*, *Moving Pictures*, *Things Seen*, *Imaginary Museum*, *A Field Guide to the Wildlife of Suburban Oahu*, *Cardinal Points*, and *What the Kite Thinks*. His other sorts of books include *Looking for Edward Gorey*, *The Important Books: Children's Picture Books as Art and Literature*, and *Stan Musial: A Biography*. His poems have appeared in *Poetry*, *New Letters*, *Antioch Review*, *Harvard Review*, *New York Quarterly*, and many other magazines. He frequently collaborates with other poets, visual artists, playwrights, and composers. He occasionally teaches poetry workshops, such as the "Starting with Art" workshops he has taught at Poets House (in New York City) and at the Honolulu Museum of Art. He is Professor Emeritus of Art History and American Studies at the University of Hawaii at Manoa.

Claire Taylor is a writer in Baltimore, Maryland. She is the author of a children's literature collection, *Little Thoughts*, as well as two micro-chapbooks: *A History of Rats* (Ghost City Press, 2021), and *As Long as We Got Each Other* (ELJ Editions, 2022). You can find her online at clairemtaylor.com and Twitter @ClaireM_Taylor.

Ingrid L. Taylor is a poet, essayist, and veterinarian whose poems have most recently appeared in the *Southwest Review*, *Ocotillo Review*, *Collateral*, and others. She has received *Punt Volat Journal*'s Annual Poetry Award, is a Pushcart nominee, and was a featured poet in the Horror Writers Association's *Annual Poetry Showcase,* vol. 8. Her nonfiction has appeared in *HuffPost*, *Sentient Media*, and *Feminist Food Journal*. She has been awarded support for her writing from the Playa

Artist Residency, the Horror Writers Association, and Gemini Ink. Find out more about her work at ingridltaylor.com.

Peter Taylor attends to inner landscapes in people and in words. Deeply rooted in New York City and woodland, he and his husband now make their home on a Nova Scotia bluff overlooking the North Atlantic.

Alarie Tennille was a pioneer coed at the University of Virginia, where she earned her degree in English, Phi Beta Kappa key, and black belt in Feminism. Now retired, she enjoys more time with her husband, assorted cats, and poetry. She serves on the Emeritus Board and Programming Committee of The Writers Place in Kansas City, MO. Her latest book, *Three A.M. at the Museum*, was selected as Director's Pick at the Nelson-Atkins Museum of Art. Now her book gets to spend the night at the museum. Yes, Alarie's a bit jealous. alariepoet.com

Ohio born and raised, **Kerry Trautman** is one of the founders of ToledoPoet.com and the "Toledo Poetry Museum" page on Facebook which promote Northwest Ohio poetry events. Her work had appeared in dozens of anthologies and journals such as *Slippery Elm, Free State Review, The Fourth River, Midwestern Gothic,* and *Gasconade Review*. Her poetry books are: *Things That Come in Boxes* (King Craft Press, 2012), *To Have Hoped* (Finishing Line Press, 2015), *Artifacts* (NightBallet Press, 2017), and *To be Nonchalantly Alive* (Kelsay Books, 2020), *Marilyn: Self-Portrait, Oil on Canvas* (Gutter Snob Books, 2022), and *Unknowable Things* (Roadside Press, 2023).

Mark Tulin is a former mental health professional enjoying retirement in Palm Springs. He is a Pushcart nominee and a Best of Drabble. His poetry and prose have appeared in numerous literary journals, anthologies, and podcasts. He is the author of *Magical Yogis* (Prolific Press, 2017), *Awkward Grace* (Kelsay Books, 2019), *The Asthmatic Kid and Other Stories* (Madville Publishing, 2020), *Junkyard Souls* (Alien Buddha Press, 2021), and *Rain on Cabrillo* (Cyberwit, 2021). Find Mark at Follow Mark at www.crowonthewire.com and on Twitter: @Crow_writer.

Alan Walowitz is a Contributing Editor at *Verse-Virtual, an Online Community Journal of Poetry*. His chapbook, *Exactly Like Love,* comes from Osedax Press. The full-length, *The Story of the Milkman and Other Poems,* is available from Truth Serum Press. Most recently, from Arroyo Seco Press, is the chapbook *In the Muddle of the Night*, written with poet Betsy Mars.

Amy Sage Webb-Baza is Professor of English and Director of the Creative Writing Program at Emporia State University, where she was named Roe R. Cross Distinguished Professor and directs the Donald Reichardt Center for Publishing and Literary Arts. She is managing editor for Bluestem Press and *Flint Hills Review*. She publishes fiction, poetry, and nonfiction, and is author of *Your Own Life: Kansas Stories*.

Kathleen Weed is a licensed marriage and family therapist, with advanced training in loss, grief, and meaning reconstruction. Kathleen lives and works in the San Francisco Bay Area. In addition to her therapy practice, she has led workshops for grief counselors on various therapeutic ways to incorporate poetry when working with bereaved clients. Five of her essays appear in the critically acclaimed anthology, *The Grieving Garden, Living with the Death of a Child,* co-authored and edited by Suzanne Redfern and Susan K. Gilbert, Hampton Roads Publishing Inc.

Laura Grace Weldon is the author of four books and was named 2019 Ohio Poet of the Year. She works as a book editor, teaches writing, and maxes out her library card each week. Connect with her at lauragraceweldon.com

Jon Wesick is a regional editor of the *San Diego Poetry Annual*. He's published hundreds of poems and stories in journals such as the *Atlanta Review, Berkeley Fiction Review, New Verse News, Paterson Literary Review, Pearl, Pirene's Fountain, Slipstream, Space and Time,* and *Tales of the Talisman.* Jon is the author of the poetry collections *Words of Power, Dances of Freedom* and *A Foreigner Wherever I Go* as well as several novels and short story collections. His most recent novel is *The Prague Deception.* http://jonwesick.com

Fred Zirm is a retired English and drama teacher who still directs plays at community theaters near his home in Rockville, Maryland. His poems, flash fiction, and creative non-fiction have been published in more than a dozen journals and anthologies. His chapbook, *Object*

Lessons, was published in January 2021 by Main Street Rag Publishing Company.

www.ingramcontent.com/pod-product-compliance
Lightning Source LLC
Chambersburg PA
CBHW031633160426
43196CB00006B/396